Contents

Content Guidance

What is a caucus? • What is a primary? • Key terms associated with primaries • How important are the national nominating conventions? • What are the key features of the presidential campaign? • How important are the media in election campaigns? • Campaign finance • What is the Electoral College and how does it work? • The use of direct democracy in the USA • What are recall elections? • Some comparative features of UK electoral processes

How do the parties differ? • Internal coalitions • Party organisation • Party decline and party renewal • The two-party system in the USA • Comparison with UK parties

Partisan alignment • Partisan de-alignment • Abstention in US elections • Some comparisons with the UK

What is a pressure group? • What are the main types of pressure group in the USA? • Why has activity grown in recent years? • How do pressure groups achieve their aims? • Access points in the political system • What are the most important factors affecting the success of pressure groups? • What 'outsider' strategies are pursued by US pressure groups? • Are pressure groups a threat to democracy? • Are there checks to pressure group power? • Political action committees • Comparisons with UK pressure groups

Questions & Answers

Getting the most from this book

Questions & Answers

Exam-style questions

Examiner comments on the questions
Tips on what you need to do to gain full marks, indicated by the icon ⓔ.

Sample student answers
Practise the questions, then look at the student answers that follow each question.

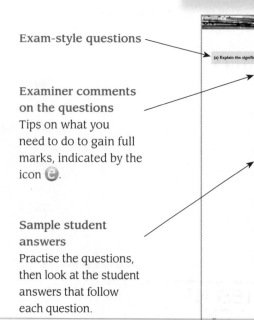

Examiner commentary on sample student answers
Find out how many marks each answer would be awarded in the exam and then read the examiner comments (preceded by the icon ⓔ) following each student answer. Annotations that link back to points made in the student answers show exactly how and where marks are gained or lost.

About this book

This guide has been written to help students opting for AQA Unit 3A, The Politics of the USA, to prepare more effectively. Its aim is to provide students with a clear outline of the way in which the unit is structured and examined, as well as a summary of the content for each part of the unit. Unit 4A, The Government of the USA, is covered in a separate unit guide.

How to use this guide

The Content Guidance section looks at the core content of the unit, focusing on the four areas covered in the specification, including key concepts and theories. The greater focus at A2 on analysis and evaluation is stressed, as well as the need for the effective use of evidence and examples to back up arguments.

The Questions and Answers section covers assessment objectives and levels of response at A2, and advice on achieving examination success. Student responses to examination questions at A2 are included, explaining why students gain, or fail to gain, higher-level marks for their responses and how examination responses could be improved to achieve higher marks and grades.

Although no previous knowledge of US government is required in this unit, it may be useful to you to have some outline knowledge of the way in which US government is structured especially through the constitution, to aid contextual awareness and general understanding of the unit. Similarly, it will be beneficial at the beginning of the course for you to have some basic knowledge of the USA itself, such as key events in its history, its size and socioeconomic, ethnic, religious and regional diversity, its changing demographics and its dominant values, to provide a useful context for understanding its politics.

Specification at a glance

The AQA Unit 3A specification below shows in more detail the key concepts associated with each of the four parts of the unit. It also provides helpful amplification of the core content of the unit as a guide for studying, revision and exam practice.

The electoral process and direct democracy

Key concepts	Content and amplification
<ul><li>Open, closed and 'invisible' primaries</li><li>The caucus system</li><li>Balanced ticket</li><li>Candidate and issue-centred campaigns</li><li>Momentum</li><li>Soft and hard money</li><li>Negative campaigning</li><li>Insider and outsider candidates</li><li>Fixed terms</li><li>Swing states</li></ul>	<ul><li>The main characteristics of presidential and congressional elections and the main influences on their outcomes</li><li>Candidate selection and nomination through the primary and caucus system and the role of the national nominating conventions</li><li>Debates concerning the workings and outcomes of the Electoral College and its impact on campaigns</li></ul>

Key concepts	Content and amplification
	• The significance of money as a factor in electoral success and the impact of the media on campaigns and candidates • Direct democracy at state level through the use of referendums, initiatives, propositions and recall elections, and debates concerning their use • Comparisons with the UK electoral process to illustrate arguments

Political parties

Key concepts	Content and amplification
• Liberalism • Conservatism • Big tent parties • Internal coalitions • Neo-liberal and neo-conservative • New right • Religious right • Compassionate conservatism	• The two main political parties and their differing ideologies, values, policies and traditions • The factionalised nature of the parties: the reasons for, and consequences of, their internal divisions • Party organisation • Recent changes to the parties and reasons for these changes • Debates over party decline or renewal • Debates concerning the weakness of US parties • Reasons for two-party dominance and the significance of third parties and independent candidates • Comparisons with UK parties to illustrate arguments

Voting behaviour

Key concepts	Content and amplification
• Partisanship • Alignment and de-alignment • Gender gap • New Deal Coalition • Democratic overload • Differential abstention • Ticket splitting • Swing voters	• Consideration of the main variables affecting the way people vote in the USA and their relative importance • The long-term determinants of American electoral behaviour including socioeconomic status, gender, age, race and ethnicity, region and religion • The significance of partisan alignment and de-alignment • Links between the parties and their core voting coalitions • Recency factors in voting behaviour including different issues and candidates at different elections and their relative importance • Factors causing change in voting behaviour • The causes and consequences of split-ticket voting and high levels of abstention • Comparisons with UK voting behaviour to illustrate arguments

Key concepts	Content and amplification
• Pluralism • Elitism • Lobbying • Access points • Single-issue groups • Corporate power • Direct action • Iron triangles • Clientelism	• The meaning of political pluralism and debates about its extent in the USA • Types and classification of pressure groups, including economic, moral, environmental, ethnic, gender and issue-based groups • Sectional and cause groups • Debates concerning the methods and tactics used by pressure groups to influence decision making and the reasons for success or lack of it • The relative power of pressure groups vis-à-vis political parties • Controversies over the extent of pressure groups' power in the USA • The role and significance of political action committees, especially regarding electoral finance • Comparisons with UK pressure groups to illustrate arguments

How to do well in Unit 3A

It is important to recognise that A2 units are more demanding than AS units. After a year of studying politics, however, the groundwork has been covered, so that the greater A2 challenges can be faced with confidence.

Make sure that you are very familiar with the Unit 3A specification, including:
- the four areas of the unit content on which questions will be based
- the number of questions on the paper and the marks for each section
- the choice of questions and the type of questions
- the assessment objectives and the levels of response

You can get a copy of the AQA specification through the website **www.aqa.org.uk**. This includes examiners' reports on previous exams, mark schemes and the generic assessment criteria, which should guide your studies.

Read

From day 1, be prepared to read widely around the subject to broaden and deepen your knowledge of American politics and American political issues. Reading should include:
- UK and US quality newspapers and websites and their coverage of American politics as it happens. Using these resources can be particularly rewarding in terms of picking up contemporary evidence and examples
- up-to-date textbooks on American politics
- articles in *Politics Review* that are focused on specific topics, which should be used to reinforce your class notes

- current affairs journals such as *Time* or *Newsweek* and *The Economist* (which includes an excellent American Survey section) which have extensive coverage of American political issues that should stimulate as well as inform
- A. J. Bennett's *US Government and Politics Annual Update*, published by Philip Allan.

Watch

Watch the television news regularly, paying special attention to American political stories as they happen, to update your notes.

Note

Use notebooks to record significant American political developments and issues, otherwise some key changes and events that take place while you are studying and are not in your textbooks will be forgotten. These notes can be a very effective supplement to your textbook and class notes.

File

Try to keep an organised file from the beginning, filing your notes in an order that makes sense to you and can be understood by you. It is then possible to summarise these notes on index cards during your intensive revision programme at the end.

Review

It is important to review your notes on a regular basis — this means you are learning as you go along, avoiding last-minute panics. Revision means revisiting, but this should be revisiting specification topics that you already know, not trying to learn them from scratch for the examinations. Last-minute panic revision of topics not fully understood should always be avoided, as it is rarely successful.

Reduce your notes to manageable proportions

It helps to rewrite or reformat your notes and you can transfer all the key points that need to be known onto revision index cards, with one card for each part of a topic. This will make learning much more manageable.

Study and revise all four areas of the unit

Remember, there are no predictable questions in examinations, and if you study and revise selectively, leaving large gaps in your overall knowledge and understanding of American politics, it could be disastrous for your result. Work to understand all four areas of the unit as laid out in the specification and to see any important links between them.

Content Guidance

This section of the guide aims to address the key areas of content in the four sections of the AQA Unit 3A specification: elections and direct democracy, political parties, voting behaviour and pressure groups. It focuses on the main theories, issues and debates in these four areas and explains the key concepts, highlighted in green, that need to be known and understood. Although there are no comparative questions for the unit, reference is made to comparative features in the UK political system, to facilitate the synoptic understanding required at A2. While making no claim to cover every possible aspect of the four specification areas in detail, the content guidance aims to provide concise but thorough coverage of the core topics. This material is best used as the basis for further in-depth study and your own independent research to find additional examples and evidence from other sources and from contemporary developments in the ever-changing politics of the USA.

The electoral process and direct democracy

The US electoral process operates in the context of the following constitutional provisions:
- a federal structure, with different layers of government
- a separation of powers, with different branches of government
- fixed terms of office for all elected positions

These can only be changed by constitutional amendment. This system results in 'permanent' campaigns and a sense of 'democratic overload', with more than 100,000 elections taking place annually in over 80,000 units of government, for a wide range of posts from the president to the local dog-catcher.

In the USA, candidates for office are not chosen by the parties, but by voters in primaries and caucuses. This is the nomination process, which takes place every 4 years for the presidential election and every 2 years for the mid-term congressional elections. It is the government of each state that decides whether to hold caucuses or primaries.

Knowledge check 1

How does the constitutional federal structure and separation of powers affect the US electoral process?

What is a caucus?
- Caucuses are a series of state-based meetings of party activists who come together to indicate their preferences for the candidates. They have been termed 'low-turnout high-intensity' elections.
- They are found in less densely populated states, such as Nevada. The caucus in Iowa is the first and is traditionally regarded as the most important, because of

momentum Nicknamed the 'big mo', momentum refers to surges in support after wins in the invisible primary, early primaries and caucuses. It can lead to advantages over rivals, such as more media attention, name and face recognition, donors, voters 'jumping on the bandwagon' and often front-runner status. Candidates who fail to achieve or sustain momentum may drop out early.

Knowledge check 2

Which kinds of state hold caucuses, who votes in them and with what results?

Knowledge check 3

What is the significance of the invisible primary?

Examiner tip

The reasons for the use of state primaries and caucuses, their characteristics and their outcomes are different, so always use examples of the results of primaries and caucuses to provide evidence of differences.

the **momentum** it gives to the winning candidate, as was the case, for example, with Barack Obama in 2008. The same was true in 2012 for the Republican contest when Mitt Romney won the initial caucus elections by a very slim margin of just eight votes.

- Before the 1960s, most states held caucuses, but now only a minority do. Caucus voters are likely to be more extreme activists (to the left in the Democratic Party and to the right in the Republican Party), operating in the 'smoke-filled room' style of machine politics. Caucuses, therefore, are less democratic than primaries.
- Caucus results are not representative of the opinions of the wider party or electorate, and turnout tends to be very low. Nowadays, to win the nomination, a candidate must win primaries as well as caucuses.

What is a primary?

- Primaries are intra-party state elections to select the party's nominee for the presidential election, and are now held in the majority of states. Rules for their use are decided by the states themselves and also by the Democratic and Republican parties within those states.
- Like caucuses, primaries do not actually elect the candidate, but select delegates to attend the national nominating convention, where they cast a vote for 'their' candidate. The winner of the popular vote in the state primary receives delegates by a winner-takes-all process or by some form of proportional representation, depending on state and party rules.
- Larger states have more delegates and are therefore important to win.
- There are different types of primary elections: open and closed. In an open primary, any voter can vote in either party's primary (but not in both), while in a closed primary only registered party voters may participate.

Key terms associated with primaries

- **The invisible primary.** This is the period after candidates declare their intention to run and before the Iowa caucus and New Hampshire primary, when candidates try to achieve advantages over their rivals, such as greater name and face recognition, funding (building up a 'war chest') and momentum.
- **Front-loading.** This is the term used when states bring forward their primaries in an attempt to achieve more influence over the outcome.
- **The New Hampshire primary.** New Hampshire is famous as the first state to hold its primary and for the momentum this can give to candidates despite its small and unrepresentative character. Until Bill Clinton in 1992, every president had won this primary, but since then it has been a less reliable predictor of the winner. For example, Obama lost to Hillary Clinton in 2008. Mitt Romney, however, won the Republican primary there in January 2012 and went on to secure the nomination.
- **Super Tuesday.** Traditionally, this is when large numbers of states hold their primaries on the same day. The actual date varies though from election cycle to election cycle. In 2012 it took place on 6 March when ten states held their Republican primaries, fewer than in 2008. It has sometimes proved to be a key turning point in a candidate's fortunes, as was the case of John McCain in 2008.

AQA A2 Government & Politics

What is the case *for* the use of primaries?

- Primaries provide more democratic choice for voters, ending 'smoke-filled room' politics and control by party bosses who are not representative of the wider party.
- They show who can win and where. Primaries produce candidates with national appeal who can win in different regions of the country. For example, Clinton in 1992 was a southern Democrat who showed he had appeal in the northern liberal states, while Obama in 2008 was a northern liberal who showed that he could win in the conservative south.
- Primaries weed out weaker candidates with little chance of winning the presidential election: such candidates fail to gain or sustain momentum as the primary campaigns progress. In the 2012 Republican primaries, 'Queen of the Tea Party' candidate Michele Bachmann dropped out straight after the Iowa caucus where she came sixth.
- The long and gruelling nature of the primaries tests the stamina and character of the candidates and therefore their suitability for the presidency.

What is the case *against* the use of primaries?

- They go on for too long. The invisible primary effectively creates a situation of permanent campaigning, which causes many voters to lose interest.
- The constant media focus increasingly including televised debates, tends to trivialise the process, emphasising 'beauty contest' image rather than 'policy' substance.
- The huge cost of campaigning means that candidates spend an excessive amount of time fund-raising. Candidates who lack funds or face a well-financed rival may have to drop out, regardless of their qualities as potential presidents.
- Candidates can become exhausted by relentless travelling and campaigning under a 24/7 media spotlight, particularly when they already hold demanding political office.
- Primaries can give momentum to **outsider candidates** with little experience of governing and no substantial preparation for the presidency. (This does not necessarily mean, of course, that such a candidate will not make a good president.)
- Primaries reduce the party's role in selecting its presidential nominee, as candidates create personal campaign organisations, raise finance and run on their personality and views, with little peer review from party insiders.
- Primaries are divisive contests, as candidates from the same party attack and try to discredit each other, making it difficult to reunite the party to fight the real contest in November. This happened in 1992 to the Republican Party, and George Bush Senior lost the subsequent election.
- Because of low turnout, primaries can lead to unrepresentative results.
- To win primaries, Republican candidates must move to the right to appeal to their base of core voters, whereas Democratic candidates must move to the left. They then have to pull the campaign back into the middle ground to fight the real election, thus potentially alienating voters and leading to accusations of 'flip-flopping' regarding their policies.

Knowledge check 4

Why have primaries been described as 'political Darwinism?'

outsider candidates
This term refers to a candidate's lack of experience of Washington DC politics. Many outsider candidates are state governors who 'run against Washington politics' such as Jimmy Carter, Ronald Reagan and George W. Bush. Insiders like George Bush stress Washington experience of how the system works. Outsider candidates like George W. Bush may choose a Washington insider to balance the ticket, such as Dick Cheney who had previously been defense secretary.

Examiner tip
There is no agreement on whether the use of primaries or caucuses is the best process to select the presidential candidates. Understand the debate over both the democratic advantages and the disadvantages of these selection methods.

How important are the national nominating conventions?

The national nominating conventions are slick media spectacles run by the parties' national committees, and they conclude the nomination process. They have become less important in recent years, as the results are already known beforehand from the primaries. As a result, the main role of the national nominating convention is now to 'crown' the candidate rather than to choose the candidate, as it did in the past.

Although the conventions have lost their formal function to decide the parties' presidential nominees, they retain several important informal functions:

- The convention ratifies the party's official nominee, and after the acceptance speech the party has the opportunity to unite around the chosen candidate and heal political wounds from the campaign — as happened in 2012 with the Republicans.
- The convention is the only time the party meets nationally, bringing together delegates from 50 state parties and the party's super-delegates — the party officials and elected representatives who are not pledged or bound by primary or caucus votes. After the convention, the party effectively reverts to 50 state parties.
- The party platform, its official set of policy positions, is adopted at the national nominating convention, in a way similar (but not identical) to the adoption of a party manifesto in the UK. These platform policies will already have been put forward in the winning candidate's primary campaign, so in effect the convention is now endorsing them rather than determining them.
- The presidential candidate hopes to achieve a 'bounce' in the polls after the convention as a result of extensive media coverage and a national platform. This has been less true lately though. In 2012 Romney actually went *down* 1% in polls after the convention, while Obama only rose 3%. Back in 2000 by contrast, both candidates gained 8% post convention.
- It used to be the opportunity to announce the vice-presidential candidate. But in 2012 unusually, Romney named Paul Ryan as his running mate 16 days before the Republican convention. The choice of nominee is important for providing a balanced ticket — the vice-presidential nominee will have characteristics not possessed by the presidential candidate, which it is hoped will widen their appeal to voters. Obama's selection of Biden in 2008 balanced his race, age and lack of Washington experience, and was aimed at attracting the white, male, blue-collar vote. Romney's choice of the conservative Wisconsin congressman Paul Ryan in 2012, helped to shore up support with Tea Party Republicans suspicious of Romney's relatively moderate record as governor of liberal-inclined Massachusetts.

What are the key features of the presidential campaign?

Once the balloons come down on delegates at the end of the nominating convention, the candidate and party gear up for the national campaign, starting officially on Labor Day, the first Monday in September.

Knowledge check 5

Why do 'political wounds' have to be healed at the conventions?

Knowledge check 6

Explain the role of the super-delegates in the Democratic Party.

balanced ticket
Presidential nominees wish to select a vice-president with different characteristics from their own to maximise their vote by appealing to different types of voter. The ticket can be balanced ideologically, geographically, ethnically or by factors such as gender, age, religion or experience. Each choice will show different factors at work.

Examiner tip
Be aware of the importance of the conventions in ending the nomination process in the states and launching the national campaign, and be able to distinguish between their formal and informal functions.

In the presidential campaign, the candidate must try to influence more than 200 million voters, in 50 states of variable electoral importance. They will target their campaign strategy, aided by armies of specialist advisers whose job is to help them win the biggest prize, control of the executive branch of government. To do this they must:

- 'energise the base': enthuse their core, aligned voters to turn out to vote
- win over the independent voters whose votes are not yet decided — a difficult balancing act
- create momentum for the campaign by raising funds and creating an electoral bandwagon

In their campaign strategy, they must take into account the following factors:

- The huge size of the USA and the diversity of the voters.
- The need to win Electoral College votes by focusing on key 'swing states' such as Ohio, Florida and Pennsylvania, ruthlessly targeting them with campaign funds and political advertising. Candidates will tend to ignore states they know they can win and those they are bound to lose.
- The need to target 'swing voters' in key states, such as the elderly in Florida or industrial workers in Ohio, with specific messages. At the same time they must target the women's vote, the youth vote, the Hispanic vote and other groups, which can cause problems in terms of what to say, where and to whom in order to win votes (or not lose them).
- Candidates can no longer rely on large numbers of aligned voters always turning out to vote for their party.
- The 'incumbency effect'. An incumbent president can have an advantage through being perceived as looking more 'presidential' than the challenger. This did not, however, help incumbents Jimmy Carter in 1980 and George H. W. Bush in 1992, when other factors were important in explaining their defeat. This effect is more significant in congressional elections, where incumbent senators and representatives can gain significant electoral advantage by, for example, claiming credit for securing federal funding for local 'pork-barrel' projects. Obama's re-election in 2012 was unusual in that he was almost unique among US presidents in being re-elected with a smaller share of the vote than in his first term.

Candidates make appeals to voters on the basis of:

- the party identification of the voters: the candidate's Democratic or Republican label is the voting cue for aligned voters
- their personal characteristics, such as likeability or trustworthiness, and their experience: voters often vote for the candidate rather than for the party
- the policy positions that they take on important salient political issues, especially on the economy

Finally, candidates attempt to connect with voters and persuade them through:

- old-style whistle-stop campaigns, visiting key states and making speeches
- debates on television
- focus groups
- political advertising through the mass media and modern technology such as the internet

---

Knowledge check 7

Give examples of the 'specialist advisers' who run presidential campaigns.

swing states Also called 'battleground states', these are states that can be won or lost by either candidate, unlike blue (Democrat) or red (Republican) 'safe states'. There are though increasingly fewer true 'swing states'. In 2012, only four states were won by a margin of less than 5%: Ohio, Virginia, North Carolina and Florida. Candidates focus their campaigns in these states with constant advertising and frequent visits.

In order to win the presidency, candidates must use the above to build broad coalitions of voters, who will vote through the medium of the Electoral College, within the fixed terms laid down by the constitution.

How important are the media in election campaigns?

The mass media are now the main channel of political communication enabling candidates to connect to voters. The first election in which television was a major factor was in 1960, when John Kennedy's television image was seen as the key factor in his success over the less media-friendly Richard Nixon.

The media have four main influences on campaigns:

- They personalise campaigns, tending to focus on image and appearance rather than policy positions, on style rather than substance. It is said that Abraham Lincoln's appearance would make him unelectable in modern politics. It is also argued that media focus changes the types of candidate coming forward, as well as their style of campaigning. Candidates are marketed on the basis of their looks, personalities and personal views, with little focus on the party in whose name they stand.
- Elections are now held under 24/7 media coverage. Campaigns are run by experienced media advisers and pollsters who use focus groups and 'voter meters' to test voter reaction to candidates and what they are saying. Candidates will often shift their views in response to professional consultations with key groups in the electorate.
- There is increasing emphasis on photo-opportunities on prime-time television, often engineered to get coverage in the free media, such as news channels like Fox, CNN and MSNBC, rather than relying on the paid media of television advertising. Candidates compete to coin the best sound bites to capture the attention of the electorate, such as Obama's 'Yes we can'. Everything is planned to come across well on television, which helps candidates who are good media performers, such as Ronald Reagan.
- Cable networks are used to send highly targeted messages in order to influence groups of voters. For example, the conservative 'shock jock' radio channels with hosts such as Glenn Beck can influence voters on the right.

The influence of television advertising on the campaign

- Buying television advertising time is very expensive, and this is the main reason why candidates need to raise huge amounts of campaign finance.
- What is seen or heard in the media rarely persuades voters to switch their vote, but it reinforces views the voter already has. Advertising is therefore used to 'energise the base' rather than to attempt to convert votes.
- There is increasing use of **negative campaigning**, especially 'attack ads' — advertisements attacking opponents rather than putting forward positive messages. Although it is widely criticised, the reason why negative campaigning is used is that it works and is hard to counteract. It often involves painting opponents as uncaring about ordinary Americans. For example, in 2012 Romney was portrayed as a vulture capitalist directly responsible for closing down factories while working at Bain Capital.

How important are the 'great debates'?

The term used for the face-to-face broadcast encounters between the two rival candidates is a misnomer since they are arguably neither great nor debates. The first was in 1960, between John F. Kennedy, who was deemed to have won by the television viewers, and Richard Nixon, who was deemed to have won by the radio listeners, which suggests that in the end image can trump what is actually said.

The debates are now hugely stage-managed and the candidates try to score points against each other. In 2012, the lacklustre performance of Obama in the first debate gave a temporary boost to the Republicans and caused Obama to prepare and perform far better in the other debates. Most candidates tend to 'play safe', so television debates are rarely decisive in the final outcome.

Campaign finance

American campaigns have become increasingly expensive. Over $2 billion in 2012 was spent on the presidential campaign alone. It is said in the USA that 'money doesn't talk, it shouts', and that 'America has the best democracy money can buy'. A vital factor in a candidate's success in the primaries is whether he or she can amass a huge campaign war chest. This gives them a major advantage over less well-financed candidates, but also works to deter challengers who cannot raise the finance to make or sustain a bid for the presidency.

Why is money so important in US campaigns?

Finance is important in electoral campaigns for a number of reasons, including:
- the high cost of television advertising to reach voters
- the size of the country and consequently the high costs of travel and accommodation in 50 states
- the diversity of voters to whom the candidates have to appeal with highly targeted messages
- the need to hire specialist staff to run a modern campaign, including the use of new technology
- the permanent nature of campaigning, with the build-up for the next election starting the day after the last one ends

Where do candidates get their campaign finance from?

Candidates' finance comes primarily from:
- their own pockets — so it helps to be a multi-millionaire
- political action committees (PACs)
- national and congressional party committees
- 501/527 groups and Super PACs raising money to spend on issue advocacy on behalf of candidates
- fund-raising through the internet and social media, generating large numbers of small donations, as practised with great success by the Obama campaign in 2008
- federal funding **if** they agree to limit their spending. Obama took the risk of rejecting this source of funds in 2008. Both candidates rejected it in 2012 on the gamble (proved correct) that they could raise more money overall through their own efforts.

Knowledge check 10

Why are candidates now likely to reject federal funding for their campaigns?

hard money Regulated money, contributed directly to a candidate, subject to limits, monitored by the Federal Election Commission and intended to prevent the 'buying' of elections.

soft money Unregulated money, usually given to parties for 'general political activities', but banned in 2002. It now refers to money not subject to FECA restrictions or limits, usually given to groups for 'issue advocacy'.

Efforts to control the cost of US elections

There have been two main legislative attempts to limit the costs of political campaigning in the States both of which have proved largely unsuccessful. These are:

- the **Federal Election Campaign Act (FECA) 1971** (amended in 1974)
- the **Bipartisan Campaign Reform Act (BCRA) 2002 (McCain–Feingold)**

The main terms of FECA:

- It introduced federal funding for presidential (but not congressional) elections, with matching funds provided for candidates in the primaries who could raise lots of small contributions in at least 20 states.
- Federal funding is offered to each presidential candidate. If candidates accept federal funds, as John McCain did in 2008, they must agree to spending limits on their campaign. Alternatively, if they want to raise unlimited amounts of money to spend on their campaign, they can choose to reject federal funding, as Barack Obama did in 2008.

As a result of FECA, all contributions to candidates must be disclosed and supervised by the Federal Election Commission (FEC), making the process open and transparent. Also, limits are placed on all direct contributions to candidates, the so-called hard money of US politics.

The main terms of the BCRA:

- It banned all soft money contributions to candidates or parties and increased the upper limit for hard money donations from individuals to $2,000 (now $2,500) and $25,000 to a political party.
- It introduced the so-called 'stand by your ad' clause, which required all political ads to include an explicit statement about who paid for the advert, and the words often heard along the lines of 'I'm Mitt Romney [or whoever] and I approve this ad'. This enables voters to know the source of the advert.
- Private bodies such as trade unions, corporations and citizens' groups, were not allowed to run ads in the 60 days before the presidential election.

Why have attempts to limit campaign expenditure been largely unsuccessful?

- Serving politicians do not want to jeopardise their own chances of re-election, which has often depended on raising larger sums than their defeated opponents.
- The 1st Amendment of the US Constitution, which guarantees freedom of speech, has been interpreted by the courts as including political fund-raising as a form of political expression.
- Supreme Court cases. Although most of FECA was upheld in *Buckley* v *Valeo* (1976) and much of the BCRA by *McConnell* v *FEC* 2003, the *Citizens United* case in 2010 dealt a serious blow to campaign finance reform (see below). The less well-known 2011 case *Arizona Free Enterprise Club* v *Bennett,* also limited the scope of individual states to control campaign spending.
- Loopholes to both measures were quickly found and led to the increase of soft money and PACs after FECA, and the growth of 527 groups after the BCRA. 527s are named after a section of the US tax code which allows organisations to raise and spend unlimited amounts of money for 'general political activities', although they

are not allowed to coordinate their activities (usually television advertising) with the candidate or party they are supporting. A famous example of the 527s was the Swift Boat Veterans for Truth group, which funded an advert attacking Kerry's war record of bravery in order to neutralise his advantage over Bush (an alleged draft dodger). The ad was aired almost constantly and effectively in key states before the 2004 election. As Justices Stevens and O'Connor wrote in their opinions on the McConnell case in 2003: 'Money like water will always find an outlet.'

FEC v Citizens United and the new 'Super PACs'

This controversial 5/4 decision by the Supreme Court in January 2010, based on the free speech provisions of the 1st Amendment, blew a huge hole in attempts to regulate campaign spending by law.

The decision allows corporations, unions and individuals to make unlimited donations to partisan groups, now known as Super PACs, which then campaign for or against electoral candidates. (Unlike traditional PACs, they cannot directly donate any hard money to candidates.) The decision has led to an even greater influx of special interest money in campaigns, such as the spending of $75 million in 2010 by the US Chamber of Commerce to target for defeat lawmakers who had voted for healthcare reform. In the 2012 presidential campaign, Super PAC spending was around $570 million with the biggest spender being the pro-Romney group, Restore Our Future, which spent $142 million, much of it on television ads.

Although the new Super PACs can receive and spend unlimited amounts of money, they cannot coordinate their spending with either parties or candidates, but can spend 'on behalf of' them using 'independent expenditures' for 'issue advocacy'. Obama has described them as a 'threat to democracy' because of the increasing amount of money spent by them in campaigns and their likely influence over campaign outcomes. Another criticism is that, although Super PACs must disclose their donors to the FEC, there is a loophole which allows the groups to link with advocacy groups such as the new '501(c)' groups (also named after a section of the tax code) which can raise unlimited amounts of money to spend supporting or opposing candidates, but which do not have to disclose their donors.

How important is finance to a candidate's chances of success?

A key question in US politics is whether candidates, or special interests who spend on their behalf, can 'buy' electoral success and also whether well-funded candidates have an unfair advantage over poorer rivals: there are arguments on both sides of the debate. It is possible though to find very rich candidates who have lost, such as the Republican candidate in 2010 for governor of California, Meg Whitman (ex-CEO of eBay), who spent $144m of her own fortune and still lost. There are several other factors that are important in a candidate's electoral success, such as their policies, record and image, and the circumstances of the time.

Another question is whether, in a country with rights guaranteed by the constitution's 1st Amendment, it could ever be possible to limit campaign spending effectively by law. In summary, while money does not guarantee victory in US elections, without a well-funded campaign, a candidate is at a significant disadvantage, especially if he or she is facing a well-funded incumbent.

What is the Electoral College and how does it work?

- The Electoral College is a constitutional mechanism designed to 'filter the people's will' and to elect the president indirectly. It was the result of a compromise reached in 1787, when large and small states disagreed over how the president should be elected.
- Candidates need to win the Electoral College vote (ECV), not necessarily the popular vote, to become president.
- ECVs are allocated to states according to their congressional representation: the two senators from each state plus the number of congressional districts within the state, which reflects the size of the state's population. This means the states with smaller populations have few ECVs (seven states have only 3 votes) and the larger states have more.
- The number of ECVs per state is re-apportioned every 10 years following the census to reflect changes in population between states. This was last done in 2010 when a number of states either gained or lost ECVs. For example, Florida gained 2 votes while New York lost 2. California still has the largest number with 55 ECVs.
- The total number of ECVs is fixed at 538, made up of 100 votes from Senate representation, 435 from House representation and 3 from Washington DC.
- Candidates need 270 ECVs to win.
- The last deadlocked vote in the Electoral College was in 1824, but the potential for a 269–269 vote is always there. In that event, the House of Representatives chooses the president, and the Senate selects the vice-president.
- The Electoral College follows a winner-takes-all system. In the majority of states the winner of the popular vote takes all that state's Electoral College votes regardless of the margin of the vote. So, if a candidate wins the popular vote in Ohio with a vote of 51% he or she gets all of Ohio's 18 ECVs. Maine and Nebraska allocate their ECVs slightly differently, awarding their 'House votes' on the basis of individual congressional districts won, with the 'Senate votes' going to the overall winner across the whole state. Voters actually elect a slate of electors who will deliver their votes in the state capital the following month.
- The device of the Electoral College is linked to federalism, as a presidential election is actually 50 separate contests in the 50 states (plus Washington DC) on the same day.

Knowledge check 12

How can a presidential candidate lose the popular vote yet win the presidential election, as happened in 2000?

Examiner tip

You must be clear and precise when explaining how and why the Electoral College works in the way it does, always using accurate figures as evidence.

What are the effects of the Electoral College on the campaign?

The main effect of the Electoral College system is on the campaign strategies of candidates: they will usually concentrate on the 'swing' battleground states, especially those with large ECVs, rather than the ones they either can't win or can't lose. Candidates rarely campaign in every state (as Nixon did in 1960, losing to Kennedy, who won seven of the eight largest ECV states by a hair's breadth) and they often ignore large parts of the country and large numbers of voters when campaigning. This can lead to differences in turnout, as voters in some states lack an incentive to vote. Candidates focus on key swing voters in swing states, such as the elderly in Florida or blue-collar voters in Pennsylvania, in order to win.

What criticisms are made of the Electoral College and its outcomes?

- A candidate losing the national popular vote may win the Electoral College vote, as Bush did in 2000. This puts the president's mandate and legitimacy in question, as it can be seen as denying the people's will.
- The winner-takes-all system means that all ECVs go to the winner in a state (with the exception of Maine and Nebraska) regardless of the narrowness of the victory. This distorts the winner's margin of victory.
- Campaign promises tend to be targeted on swing voters in swing states to the exclusion of other 'less important' voters in safe states.
- Small states are over-represented.
- Third-party candidates can only win ECVs with a concentrated vote in a state or states, as George Wallace did in 1968 when he won five southern states. Ross Perot's 19% national share of the vote in 1992 brought him nothing, as his vote was too dispersed to win any states.
- There is a possibility of 'faithless' or 'rogue' electors. State electors are pledged but not constitutionally bound to vote for the winner of the popular vote. There are occasions when individual electors do not do this, usually because they wish to make some political point. Since the creation of the Electoral College, there have been 157 'faithless electors', the most recent one on 2004, an anonymous Democrat elector from Minnesota, who voted for Kerry's running mate John Edwards for president, probably by mistake. Such behaviour has never in fact made a difference to the outcome, but in a deadlocked Electoral College of 269–269 it could do so. Only 29 states have laws requiring their electors to be faithful to their pledged candidate.

Why has the Electoral College not been changed?

- The Electoral College system has provided political stability by electing a president with a clear majority and mandate in all but three presidential elections since the eighteenth century. The result in 2000 was an aberration.
- Demands for reform run up against the strength of the Electoral College's constitutional status and tradition. Any change is subject to a constitutional amendment, which would require super-majorities for success. Small states, such as Wyoming and Rhode Island, would probably garner enough votes in the Senate to block any such change.
- There is little public pressure for reform, and no consensus on an acceptable alternative for electing the president. A direct popular vote conflicts with the federal nature of the USA and the jealously guarded rights of the individual states.
- The working of the Electoral College is one reason for the USA's two-party duopoly, with all presidents being Democrat or Republican. The USA has a single-person executive, so there are no demands for proportional representation, unlike the UK, where the electoral system elects a government. It would require exceptional circumstances for a third party to have a significant effect on the outcome.

As a result, despite several valid criticisms, it is unlikely that the Electoral College will be reformed or abolished. To paraphrase Churchill on democracy, it could be said that 'The Electoral College is the worst way of electing the president, except for all the rest.'

Knowledge check 13

How significant are 'faithless' or 'rogue' electors?

Examiner tip

Know about the Electoral College results for at least two presidential elections and be able to use the ECV, the popular vote and any 'rogue electors' as evidence.

Examiner tip

The Electoral College can be both criticised and defended. There is no agreement on whether it should be retained, reformed or replaced. You should know the key debates over the advantages and disadvantages of these options.

Knowledge check 14

Explain the link between federalism and the retention of the Electoral College.

Examiner tip

Note that questions on direct democracy may relate to referendums and/or initiatives and/or recall elections, and the three should be clearly distinguished.

The use of direct democracy in the USA

Although the USA has never held a national referendum, there are provisions for direct democracy mechanisms in some states, dating from the early twentieth-century progressive era. These mechanisms were seen as a way of extending democracy, putting trust in people to make decisions affecting their lives. They supplement representative democracy, but do not replace it.

What is the difference between referendums and initiatives?

Referendums

Referendums are devices used to refer a specific question directly to voters. In some states, a measure passed in the state legislature does not come into effect unless it is given approval in a referendum by voters. They are therefore a top-down device, which allows a decision to receive demonstrable popular approval and greater legitimacy. All states (except Delaware) have a requirement that amendments to the state constitution be approved by referendum. They are also frequently used for bond issues as a way of raising money for state finances.

Initiatives

In some states, ballot initiatives allows citizens to initiate a proposed state law or change in the law, provided the required number of voter signatures is collected to support it through petitions (usually between 5% and 15% of the voters in a state). If this is achieved, the question (proposition) will be placed on the ballot at an election for registered voters to support or reject. Initiatives are bottom-up devices initiated by citizens, not legislators. If supported by a majority vote, the result is usually binding on the state legislature, but many successful initiatives are struck down in the courts after legal challenges (see below). There are hundreds of examples of initiative questions: they are often on moral issues such as gay marriage or abortion, but also apply to many other political issues, such as property taxes, gun control or affirmative action.

Knowledge check 15

What is meant by saying that direct democracy 'supplements but does not replace' representative democracy?

Knowledge check 16

What is meant by the descriptions 'bottom up' and 'top down' in the context of the use of direct democracy?

Famous ballot initiatives (both from California) include:
- Proposition 13 in 1978, which reduced property taxes.
- Proposition 8 in 2008, which overturned a state law allowing gay marriage. This ballot initiative was itself overturned by a Supreme Court ruling in 2013 (*Hollingsworth* v *Perry*) reminding us that ballot initiatives are not the last word and must be in accordance with the constitution as interpreted by the Supreme Court.

Arguments *for* the use of direct democracy

Examiner tip

Have at least three well-researched examples of successful initiatives being passed in the USA to use as evidence in your answers.

- Referendums and initiatives are said to express the will of the people and are the purest form of democracy.
- Voters vote to get what they want, not what their representatives think they should get.
- Referendums and initiatives encourage wider political participation and engagement with issues.
- Voters are educated on issues as views for and against are debated in campaigns through the media.

Arguments *against* the use of direct democracy

- Elected representatives make decisions after informed debates in legislatures, using their judgement as to what is best for all the people in the long term. If you don't like their decisions you can vote to remove them at the next election.
- Voters tend to vote for their own short-term interests, as in the vote to reduce property taxes in Proposition 13 in California in 1978.
- Initiatives can threaten minority/immigrant rights, such as the abolition of gay marriage in Proposition 8 in California in 2008, and a 2012 initiative in Oklahoma to end affirmative action.
- Initiatives can be passed on the basis of small, unrepresentative turnouts of voters influenced by emotive and well-financed media and pressure group campaigns. For example, the Mormon Church spent over $20 million supporting Proposition 8.
- Campaigns lead to oversimplified arguments on highly complex issues to which only a yes/no answer can be given.
- The initiative process can be manipulated by wealthy pressure groups, employing consultants to initiate the proposition and raise the signatures to put it on the ballot. Most initiatives are not initiated by ordinary citizens, but by special interest groups wanting to influence decisions in their favour.
- The opposing sides may have unequal resources and media time, which can prevent fair representation of competing opinions. Studies show the highest-spending side usually wins, while the result may only benefit special interest groups rather than the wider community.

Examiner tip

There is no agreement on the benefits of using direct democracy devices as supplements to representative democracy in some US states. Be prepared to defend and to attack both direct and representative democracy as ways of making public policy decisions.

What are recall elections?

The recall election appears to be a highly democratic device, allowing registered voters to recall an elected state or local official from office once a signature petition and evidence of corrupt or incompetent behaviour have been presented. In 2003 Gray Davis, the Democratic governor of California, was recalled by 55% of the electorate and replaced by Arnold Schwarzenegger. In another high profile recall election in 2012, the serving Republican governor of Wisconsin, Scott Walker, survived a recall election brought about by Democrat and union opposition to his policies. There are no federal recall elections, and they are rare in the States; indeed there have only been three gubnatorial recall elections in US history.

The key argument in favour of recall elections is that they make elected officials more accountable to citizens between elections and more responsive to the public's wishes. The key argument against is that the recall may be politically motivated, aimed at removing a serving politician who was not defeated in a democratic contest at the previous election.

Examiner tip

Study the recall elections of both Davis and Walker in order to understand the arguments in favour of and against the recall process.

Knowledge check 17

How are direct democracy mechanisms triggered in the states that use them?

Some comparative features of UK electoral processes

- The 1911 Parliament Act set a maximum 5-year term for Parliament, but within that limit the prime minister has chosen when to go to the country. However, as a result of the 2011 Fixed-term Parliaments Act, the governing party no longer has an advantage through controlling the election date.

- The general election is for the election of MPs only; there is no separate election of the prime minister, and the government is drawn from the majority party in a parliamentary system.
- Constituency parties choose candidates and can also deselect them.
- The party leader is elected by the parliamentary party and the mass membership (and trade unions in the Labour Party).
- There is no equivalent to the national nominating conventions, although parties hold annual conferences.
- The campaign is a national one, fought by parties with manifestos in an official 3-week campaign.
- Campaign finance is legally limited and parties cannot buy political advertising on television. Time is allocated free of charge for party election broadcasts.
- All referendums on constitutional issues have been initiated by government. There is no provision for initiatives or recall elections in the UK.

Examiner tip

Do not introduce long, artificial and especially irrelevant UK references into your answers, although they may be used in passing to show you understand differences between elections and direct democracy in both countries.

Summary

After studying this topic you should be able to:

- Put the US electoral process and direct democracy into the constitutional context of federalism, fixed terms, separation of powers and the Electoral College, which explains, in many ways, why it works the way it does.

- Understand the US electoral process as a continuous process from the invisible primary through to the results of the Electoral College vote.

- Explain the main features of the nomination process, including the invisible primary, the primary and caucus systems and their outcomes, as well as the role and importance of the national nominating conventions.

- Understand the main features of the election campaigns of the candidates, and the main factors influencing the outcome of the campaign and the success of the candidates.

- Recognise the crucial importance of campaign finance in US elections, including how candidates raise their money, what they spend it on, the changes made to it and why it has been so difficult to reform.

- Identify and explain the workings of the Electoral College system to elect the president and why

it has been retained despite several criticisms, and not abolished and replaced or fundamentally reformed.

- Explain the workings of different kinds of direct democracy found in some US states and the arguments both for and against their use.

- Make references to the UK electoral process and direct democracy where relevant.

- Recognise the key debates and competing arguments in all these areas, including:

   - whether primaries and caucuses are the best way of selecting the presidential candidates for the parties

   - whether money actually is the most important factor in a candidate's electoral success, and whether the focus on fund-raising and huge financial war chests distorts the democratic process and allows the 'buying' of elections

   - whether the Electoral College remains the best way of electing the president of the United States

   - whether direct democracy is a better way of making political decisions than representative democracy

Political parties

The United States today has a dominant two-party system based around the Democrats and Republicans. Although the Founding Fathers were suspicious of parties, factions soon emerged which eventually developed into two political parties. The parties in their current forms essentially date from the Civil War period though have evolved and adapted to changing circumstances over time. The traditional view about political parties in the USA was that they were much closer together than their class-based equivalents in the UK. They have traditionally been viewed as 'big tent' or 'catch-all' parties, containing a wide diversity of views within each party. This relative similarity was traditionally put down to a broad consensus over:

- the constitution and the political system it created
- a capitalist economic system, with a (greater or lesser) commitment to private enterprise and free markets
- the 'dominant ideology' in the USA, with (greater or lesser) commitment to individualism, liberty, equality and the American Dream

It was argued that the differences *between* the parties were often less than the differences *within* the parties. They were seen as essentially non-ideological whose primary aim was to maximise their vote in elections in order to gain office rather than to put into practice an ideological blueprint or 'ism'. It was alleged that they usually operated in the middle ground of politics, rarely straying out of this comfort zone. When they did move outside the mainstream they were heavily defeated, as was the case with the very conservative Republican Barry Goldwater in 1964 and the very liberal Democrat George McGovern in 1972. The lesson learnt from these defeats was that parties must build broad coalitions of voting support to achieve electoral success.

The old view that the two main US parties are almost indistinguishable, however, is now very oversimplified. There are now many differences between them in terms of their:

- ideologies, values and policies (what they believe in and do)
- voting support (who supports them and why)

This is often termed the *resurgence of party* or the *rise of partisanship*. Arguably, the two parties have never been so polarised or distinct from each other.

How do the parties differ?

The Democratic Party

Historically the party of the South and the pro-slavery, anti-Union party, it became the majority party from the 1930s when Roosevelt's New Deal programme led to *realignment* in US politics. The party won support from a new coalition of votes, the New Deal Coalition. This comprised:

- A 'northern wing' of minorities, urban blue-collar workers, trade unionists and liberal intellectuals.
- Its 'southern wing' of white segregationist, conservative voters who strongly identified with the party that had supported slavery and the Confederacy.

Examiner tip

Be aware that although the parties have at times appeared similar, operating in the middle ground of politics, this view of US parties has had some important readjustments, particularly since the 1980s.

Knowledge check 18

What is meant in politics by the term 'realignment'?

The strength of this voting support made the party the 'natural party of government' from the 1930s to the 1960s, when the New Deal Coalition finally broke down under the strain of holding such contradictory voting blocs together. The breaking point came after the 1964 Civil Rights and 1965 Voting Rights legislation when, as Lyndon Johnson stated at the time, the party 'signed away the South'.

Since the 1960s, the Democratic Party has only managed to win the presidency with southern candidates — Carter in 1976 and Clinton in 1992 and 1996 — but this changed with Obama's victories in 2008 and 2012. It now appears entirely possible for the Democrats to win the presidency while losing the South.

What does the Democratic Party believe in?

The Democratic Party is the more liberal party, associated with:
- a more activist, interventionist government role in regulating and managing the economy in the interests of all the people
- the introduction and development of social welfare programmes such as Medicare/Medicaid/'Obamacare' in healthcare to promote greater equality
- equal rights programmes such as civil rights, women's rights and gay rights
- a greater willingness to reform immigration laws
- commitment to federal rather than state government action
- a more 'dovish' foreign policy, internationalist in seeking diplomatic solutions to problems
- a more 'pro-choice' stance on abortion and more in favour of gun control, environmental protection and ending the death penalty

It is because of these ideological views, values and associated policy positions that the Democratic Party attracts voting support from:
- blue-collar workers, trade unionists and less affluent public sector workers attracted by its economic views
- minorities attracted by its commitment to equal rights
- city dwellers in the 'blue' states
- intellectuals and radicals attracted to its liberal agenda
- a majority of female voters in recent elections

However, the Democratic Party lost some of its voting support to the Republicans, from:
- southern white voters in the 1960s because of its commitment to civil rights
- some northern blue-collar voters in the 1970s and 1980s alienated by its perceived liberalism

The loss of this support meant that the party became a more cohesive and coherent ideologically liberal party, particularly with the shedding of the conservative South from its voting coalition. However, the Democratic Party is still internally divided on some ideological and policy positions.

What are the main divisions in the Democratic Party?

As seen with the New Deal Coalition, the Democratic Party has historically been factionalised, with a clear division into various groups. Some of the principle current factions within the party are:

---

liberalism An ideological leaning on the centre left of the political spectrum in the USA (but not left wing as in socialism). The term was first used in the 1930s to describe support for the New Deal and voters and politicians who are more politically progressive, supporting change and intervention in the political and economic system to improve citizens' lives, and creating greater equality and social justice.

Knowledge check 19

When and why did the New Deal Coalition of votes for the Democratic Party break down?

- **Blue Dog Democrats**: these are the most fiscally and/or socially conservative Democrats, found primarily in the House. They tend to represent more conservative districts, and numbered 47 in the 2009–11 session of Congress when they held the balance of power. The majority of them voted against the public option in Obama's healthcare reforms, which he was forced to abandon. Following the 2012 mid-terms though, their number of House members fell to just 15. Some lost to more conservative Republican challengers, but a few such as founding member, Tim Holden, lost to more liberal Democrats in the primaries beforehand. This is another indication of increasing polarisation *within* the two parties. A leading Blue Dog in the 2012–14 Congress is Jim Matheson from Utah.
- **New Democrat Coalition**: this centrist grouping is more socially liberal than the Blue Dogs while still being fiscally conservative (in favour of low taxes and reduced government expenditure). They also supported the invasion of Iraq in 2003. Their origins go back to the 1980s when they were the 'modernisers' of the Democratic Party, whose aim was to rid the party of the liberal tax-and-spend image that had damaged its presidential hopes. They wanted to win back the more conservative blue-collar and southern voters who had moved to support the Republican Party. They did this in 1992 and 1996 with Clinton and Gore on the ticket. Following the 2012 mid-terms, they have around 50 Congressmen and 7 senators. Among leading members in the 2012–14 Congress are senators Mary Landrieu from Louisiana and Bill Nelson from Florida.
- **Progressive Democrats**: this is a centre-left grouping within the Democrat Party founded in 2004. It has a 'dovish' approach to foreign affairs and opposed, for example, military strikes on Syria in late 2013, as well as favouring universal healthcare and a liberal social agenda. They are heirs to the anti-war liberal Democrats of the late 1960s and early 1970s such as George McGovern. They represent the largest Democrat grouping in the 2012–14 Congress. Congressional members include African–American civil rights leader congressman John Lewis from Georgia.

The Republican Party

The Republican Party, or GOP (Grand Old Party), is historically associated with northern, pro-Union, anti-slavery views. It was the majority party until the 1930s, when realignment occurred. It became the minority party in Congress until the 1994 mid-term elections and Newt Gingrich's 'Contract with America', which gave the GOP a majority in the House and Senate, lasting until 2006. It regained control of the House though not the Senate in 2010 and held it in 2012. Although holding the presidency from 1980–92 and 2000–08, it failed to defeat Obama in 2012 when it stood a good chance due to the state of the economy. Some have put this down to the party shifting too far to the right.

What does the Republican Party believe in?

The GOP is the more ideologically conservative party, with the following characteristics:
- It is committed to a free market economy as free as possible from government intervention and regulation, and supports a less active, more limited government role.

Knowledge check 20

What are the differences between the different factions within the Democrat Party?

Examiner tip

Always distinguish between liberal, conservative and moderate Democrats, their views on issues, the kind of states and districts that they represent and how they vote in Congress.

Knowledge check 21

Explain the importance of the 'Contract with America' in 1994.

conservatism An ideological leaning on the right or centre right of the political spectrum. In the USA, conservatives were so called as they opposed the New Deal and today are more likely to accept the status quo without seeking to create artificial changes to society and its institutions through government intervention or regulation.

- It is fiscally conservative, committed to lower taxes, lower spending (with the exception of defence) and balanced budgets.
- It believes the private rather than the public sector should provide employment, health and welfare (although it supports Medicare, thought to be 'untouchable', because the elderly vote in large numbers and provide a strong 'core' for the party).
- It does not support interventionist programmes to increase the rights of minority groups: its individualistic, self-help philosophy opposes the use of legislation as a way of 'artificially' creating equality.
- It is supportive of traditional family values and social and cultural conservatism.
- It is more hawkish on foreign policy issues, committed to high defence spending and the use of power to defend American interests.
- It is more committed to states' rights and the decentralisation of power.
- It takes a more 'pro-life' position on abortion and is against gun control, while supporting the death penalty and tougher immigration control.

As a result of these views and associated policies, the Republican Party has attracted voting support from:
- business and corporate interests
- higher-income voters
- white voters
- rural, small-town and suburban voters in the 'red' states
- religious groups, especially Protestants and evangelicals

What are the main divisions in the Republican Party?

Traditionally, the Republican Party was less factionalised than the Democrats, but during the Reagan presidency (1980–84 and 1984–88) ideological divisions grew between the more moderate and more conservative wings of the party. These have continued since then. Some of the groupings within the GOP are:
- **The 'liberal' wing:** moderate, fiscally conservative but socially liberal Republicans, mainly from northeastern states, representing business and corporate interests. These are known as the 'Rockefeller Republicans' or compassionate conservatives of the party. They tend to be more favourable towards abortion and gay rights for example, than most Republicans. Their influence has declined in recent years with some of their number defecting to the Democrats, including former senators Jim Jeffords and Arlen Specter. Senator Susan Collins from Maine was one of the few remaining moderate GOP senators left in the Senate after the 2012 elections.
- **The 'Main Street' or moderate wing:** this comprises the centre ground of the Republican Party and includes the presidential candidates from 2008 and 2012, Senator John McCain and Mitt Romney. They tend to be fiscally more conservative than liberals while being slightly more conservative on social issues. There is, however, a lot of variation within this informal grouping over issues such as the death penalty, gay marriage and foreign policy. Of all the factions within the GOP, they are the least easy to classify categorically.
- **The 'religious right' or neo-conservatives:** the 1980s saw the emergence of the religious right, radical right or New Right (neo-conservative) conviction-style politics associated with Reagan. This grouping is strongly conservative on social issues and is endorsed by evangelical pressure groups such as the Christian

compassionate conservatism An attempt to marry 'Rockefeller Republican', socially liberal views with the fiscally conservative views of the Republican Party. It was associated with 'softer' views on education, immigration and welfare in George W. Bush's 2000 campaign. It is seen today in the views of the small 'rump' of moderate Republicans often labelled RINOs (Republicans in name only) by their more ideologically conservative fellow Republicans.

Coalition of America. They are against abortion and gay marriage, and favour traditional family values and a strong Christian presence in the institutions of government. Like other Republicans, they are also in favour of lower taxes and a balanced budget and oppose any expansion of government welfare programmes. Perhaps paradoxically for a pro-life faction, they also tend to favour the death penalty and oppose gun control. They are strongest in the south, and leading figures in this grouping include ex vice-presidential candidate Sarah Palin and Texas governor Rick Perry. They are also generally 'hawkish' on foreign policy and support the 'Reagan/Bush Doctrine' of anti-communism and armed intervention overseas in the 'war on terror'.

- **Libertarians:** this grouping is best identified as strongly free market, in favour of minimum state intervention and the lowest possible taxes, but socially liberal on the grounds of individual liberty and often less-interventionist in foreign policy. They arguably represent the most extreme wing of the party fiscally, who are keenest to 'get the government off our backs'. Congressman Ron Paul often epitomises this strand of Republican ideology/thinking. There is some overlap with the Tea Party movement (see below).

With its newly consolidated support from the South and support from so-called 'Reagan Democrats' (blue-collar, 'Joe Six-pack' workers in the northern industrial states who switched to the Republican Party because of its more conservative positions in the 1980s) the party controversially won back the presidency in 2000, and won again in 2004. It did this by focusing on a socially conservative agenda based around the themes of 'Guns, Gays and God' and 'Faith, Flag and Family' as well as national security after 9/11. The conservative wing of the party has been ideologically dominant in Congress and the party base is highly conservative in its views. The Republicans' defeat in 2008 saw the demise of the formerly successful 'Reagan Coalition' and triggered a debate over the future direction of the party, with some fracturing along moderate and conservative ideological lines.

Related to the decline of moderates in the Republican Party is the influence of the more fiscally conservative Tea Party movement since 2009, which has served to push the Republican Party further to the right and energised the conservative grass roots, fuelled by opposition to the bailouts and growing deficits in the economy. It had an impact on Republican turnout in 2010 and the Republican primaries. There is a Tea Party caucus in the House with around 50 members led by Michelle Bachmann, and a presence in the Senate with senators Rand Paul and Tim Scott. However, while energising the base of conservative Republican voters, this may alienate more moderate, independent voters and has had little impact on the Democratic Party in moving it to the right.

Internal coalitions

It is fair to say that both parties remain 'big tent' internal coalitions, although they are distinct from one another and more united internally on principles than they were in the past. Both parties still contain a wide spectrum of ideological beliefs, and it is said that the labels 'Republican' and 'Democrat' are not accurate guides to the opinions of either voters or politicians: a prefix needs to be added, such as 'conservative', 'liberal' or 'moderate', to give the label meaning. Knowing the state, region or area that the voter or politician comes from can be a vital clue to their ideological convictions. There

---

religious right This socially conservative faction of Christian fundamentalists grew in opposition to the secularisation of the 1960s and 1970s, and particularly in reaction to the 1973 *Roe* v *Wade* decision on abortion. It now represents a large part of the base and core vote of the Republican Party. Sarah Palin was chosen as vice-presidential candidate by John McCain to boost his vote from these 'values voters' in 2008.

Examiner tip

Be able to distinguish between 'fiscal' and 'social' conservatives within the Republican Party and to give examples of the kind of issues that they support or oppose.

Examiner tip

Understand the impact that Reagan had on the Republican Party, changing its ideological direction and bringing electoral success.

Knowledge check 23

What has been the impact of the Tea Party movement on the Republican Party since 2008?

are economic conservatives and liberals, social conservatives and liberals, hawks and doves, isolationists and internationalists within each party.

Party organisation

In comparison with their counterparts in the European democracies, where parties have strong, centralised structures, the two main US political parties are weaker, decentralised structures.

Constitutional context

The reason why US parties differ from their European counterparts in their organisation is linked to constitutional provisions:

- **The separation of powers.** The executive and legislature are separate branches of government, elected separately under different mandates and designed to check and balance each other's power. This impedes the development of strong party ties both within and between the institutions.
- **Federalism.** Under a federal system, parties are organised at state level, under state law, with little control by their national committees. This means that parties and their candidates differ widely across the 50 states. In this sense, there are effectively 50 Democratic and 50 Republican parties, with a 'bottom-up' rather than 'top-down' organisation.

What other factors lead to 'weak' parties in the USA?

- They have no mass membership (though voters can register as Democrat or Republican).
- There are no party leaders as such. The president is the leader of the country rather than of his party, and there is congressional leadership only through the speaker of the house and the majority and minority leaders.
- There are no party manifestos, only 'platforms' decided at the conventions. Candidates for congressional and state office stand on their own personal views, and focus on local rather than national issues.
- The finance that candidates need in order to run for office is raised mainly by the candidates and their PACs, not their parties.
- Candidates for office are selected by primaries and caucuses rather than by the party. They can only be removed by the electorate at the next election, or through primary defeat, and cannot be deselected by their parties.

The effect of the above factors is that there is little, if any, control by the parties over their candidates running for office, and so when individuals are elected to office they tend to vote the way that they want, not how the party tells them to. In Congress there is little party discipline to control their voting.

Party decline and party renewal

Is the party over?

The debate over party decline started with David Broder's thesis in the 1970s that 'the party is over' because of the change to the parties' traditional functions.

There were five main arguments supporting the thesis.

Selection of candidates through primaries

Until the 1960s, parties selected candidates through machine politics and party bosses, but this changed with the use of primary elections, where candidates are chosen by voters, not by the party. Candidates now create personal organisations to appeal to voters and put across their personal views on issues. These intra-party contests weaken parties as candidates fight each other for nomination.

Changes to electoral finance

In most democracies, parties fund their candidates seeking election. In the USA, candidates raise 'hard money' contributions, gain funding from political action committees, or accept federal funding for presidential elections. This funding goes to the candidate, not the party, which reduces the party's organisational role in the campaign.

Changes in campaigning

Candidates now reach out to voters through the mass media and political advertising that focuses on the candidate and their image. Media campaigns strengthen candidate identification and weaken party identification, as they stress the characteristics of the candidate and play down the party. Victory is then seen as a personal, not a party, victory.

Growth of powerful interest groups and single-issue politics

US politics is now more characterised by pressure groups focusing on single issues such as abortion or the environment than by party politics.

Partisan de-alignment

Reduced attachment of voters to parties can lead to split-ticket voting, voters switching between parties, and higher abstention. Candidates make personal appeals to these independent voters to gain their votes.

However, most political commentators now write of the renewal and even resurgence of US parties, both ideologically and organisationally.

What is the evidence for ideological resurgence?

- The Republican Party is now more ideologically cohesive as a fiscally and socially conservative party. Karl Rove's strategy for Bush in 2004 and the impact of the Tea Party in 2010 energised the base of 'values voters' in order to get the core conservative voters out to the polls.
- The Democratic Party is now more ideologically cohesive and offers a clear alternative to the Republican Party, appealing to voters as a party of liberal values and policies, as seen in the 2008 campaign and support for healthcare reform, economic stimulus and banking regulation.
- Ideological cohesion is reflected in congressional voting, with greater party unity and increasing partisanship on issues. For example, no Republican voted for healthcare reform (which they call 'Obamacare') in Congress in 2010. Not a single Democrat voted against the repeal of 'Don't Ask Don't Tell' (which excluded openly gay men and women from the military). In addition, Supreme Court nomination

Examiner tip
The 'party's over' thesis is now outdated as, although US parties are still weak when compared to the centralised and disciplined UK parties, they are organisationally and ideologically stronger than when the journalist David Broder argued that they were in decline in 1971.

votes have become increasing polarised: in 2010, only five Republican senators voted to confirm Elena Kagan, while only one Democrat voted against.

Examiner tip
Have evidence of increasing party unity scores in congressional votes, showing greater partisanship and ideological polarisation. These can be found in *Congressional Quarterly*.

- There are a decreasing number of 'centrist' legislators from both parties in Congress. When they retire or are defeated, they are usually replaced by someone less moderate. For example, in 2012, Democrat moderate senator Ben Nelson of Nebraska was replaced by a more conservative Republican, Debra Fischer.
- In the 2010–12 Congress, the voting record of the most conservative Democrats was still more liberal than that of the most liberal Republicans, again showing the extent of party polarisation and greater ideological unity.
- There is less evidence of 'split-ticket' voting, where electors choose candidates from different parties for different elected offices.

Some words of caution about ideological resurgence and the growth of partisanship

It is worth noting that party unity in Congress is still somewhat weaker than at Westminster. There are still examples of some legislators voting *across* party lines:

- Eight senators broke party ranks over the gun control bill in April 2013. Four Republicans including McCain backed the bill, while four Democrats sided with the majority of Republicans and opposed it. The bill introduced in the wake of the school shootings in Connecticut, was a bi-partisan effort co-sponsored by two Democrats and two Republicans.
- 34 Democrats in the House voted against the Obamacare bill in 2010.

What is the evidence for organisational resurgence?

While the parties are generally characterised by organisational weakness, several recent developments suggest that the national party structures may be playing a greater role:

- The parties' national committees and chairs are playing an increasingly important role between elections, as well as organising the national conventions every 4 years. This can be seen in the Brock reforms in the Republican Party and the Dean reforms for the Democrats.
- National party campaigning strategies have been created to elect the president and members of Congress and state legislatures, and these involve some party control over the direction and focus of the campaigns and how the parties' resources are targeted (e.g. the Democrats' 6 for 6 campaign in 2006).
- The Republican National Committee declined to seat the full delegations of five states including Florida and South Carolina at its 2012 convention because it held its primaries earlier than allowed under new party rules.
- Both national committees now channel political donations to candidates in tight races and can withdraw finance from candidates they do not approve of.

US parties may be relatively weak in organisational terms, but there has been much evidence of party renewal and it may simply be the case that both parties have changed their role and functions rather than declined, and are simply different from what they were in the 1950s and 1960s. Rather than parties being 'over' we can conclude:

- they are both still active at and between elections
- other parties have made no significant inroads into their support

- the majority of voters still identify with them
- it is very rare for any candidate to be elected without belonging to one or the other of them

The two-party system in the USA

Despite the USA's huge social, economic, regional and ethnic diversity, it has only two parties competing for political office at all levels in all branches of government. This duopoly has existed since the beginning of the Republic and is regarded as a paradox, since there are so many deep divisions in the population and only two parties to represent that huge diversity.

Why does the USA have a two-party system?

The electoral system and 'wasted votes'

In congressional elections, the use of the winner-takes-all system in single-member districts and states leads to two-party dominance, as votes for second and third parties are always wasted.

In presidential elections, voters vote for a single executive through the Electoral College. There can only be one winner, with no possibility of power sharing in the presidency. There is nothing for the losers, no matter how many votes they gained.

'Catch-all' parties

The 'big tent' internal coalition nature of US parties and their habit of political 'clothes stealing', i.e. adopting popular policies put forward by their rivals, leaves little ideological or issue space for third parties to fill that is not already covered by the two main parties.

Partisan alignment

The party identification of most voters with the two parties is still strong, and it is difficult to establish new alignments.

A natural duopoly

On most issues there are two opposing viewpoints: for or against, left or right, liberal or conservative, and therefore there is a tendency for voters to fall into one of two camps, Democrat or Republican.

Strong pressure groups

People focused on single issues tend to form pressure groups to get their views and interests represented, rather than establishing new parties to contest elections.

Primary elections

Individuals have the opportunity through primaries to challenge candidates they disagree with, thereby giving voters a choice *within* the party, rather than requiring the formation of an alternative party. Some incumbents have lost their party's primary due to upsetting some of the 'core' by not being aligned enough with their views.

Examiner tip

Do not underestimate the changes that have taken place in the parties, both organisationally and ideologically in recent times, and be clear about the reasons for those changes.

Why are third parties not successful?

Apart from the strength of the two-party duopoly, third parties in the USA face additional difficulties.

Ballot access

Third parties face barriers in many states, such as electoral laws, which require them to gather thousands of signatures before they can get onto the ballot.

Finance

Federal funding may be given to Democrats and Republicans, but other parties only get funding if they gained 5% of the vote at the previous election. It is difficult to secure alternative sources of finance, since organisations such as political action committees want to fund winners, not losers.

Campaigning

Lack of funding means less effective campaigns. Third-party candidates find it difficult to secure media attention and coverage of their issues, and consequently struggle to achieve name recognition or national awareness. They are usually excluded from the debates and lack electoral machines to persuade their supporters to turn out to vote.

The significance of third party/independent candidates

- They can influence elections on occasion. Some argue that Ralph Nader's candidacy in 2000, when he gained 2.7% of the vote, was a factor in Gore's defeat, as he took away votes in key states such as Florida, thus handing the election to Bush. Ross Perot's 19% of the vote in 1992 was a factor in George H. W. Bush's defeat, and his platform of deficit reduction influenced both parties to adopt this position in the 1996 election. George Wallace's 1968 candidacy, when he won 46 ECVs from five southern states, could have deadlocked the Electoral College.
- A handful of independent candidates have won significant elections recently. Former Republican senator Lincoln Chaffee was elected as Governor of Rhode Island in 2011. Michael Bloomberg, having served two terms as a Republican mayor of New York, was re-elected for his third term in 2009 as an independent. It is worth noting though that both these individuals have had previous links with one of the main the parties. It also probably helps Bloomberg that a Forbes report in 2013 reckoned his personal wealth to be $27 billion. Angus King was elected as an independent senator for Maine in 2012 though he caucuses with the Democrats.

To conclude, most votes received by third parties are protest votes against the two main parties rather than positive votes for the third party concerned. It can be argued that despite their lack of electoral success, third parties have some importance within the electoral system, bringing new ideas on to the political agenda, acting as critics of the two main parties and offering a greater choice to voters. Occasionally, they even win elections.

However, none has come near to breaking the mould of American two-party politics or making an electoral breakthrough. They can never hold the balance of power or be part of a coalition, as the Liberal Democrats did in the UK Parliament after the 2010 general election. They are described as 'the bees of American politics', stinging briefly and then dying on the margin of the political system.

Comparison with UK parties

Political parties in the UK:
- have a mass membership
- have a centralised, top-down organisation
- select candidates for office at local level and can deselect MPs
- control the manifesto on which candidates for Parliament stand
- provide finance for, and direction of, the campaign
- select the leader, who becomes the prime minister or leader of the opposition, and can remove them by internal party procedures
- have strong party loyalty and party discipline through an effective whipping system

Knowledge check 25

Why are third parties referred to as 'the bees of American politics'?

Knowledge check 26

Give examples of one-party regions in the USA where one or other of the parties is dominant.

Summary

After studying this topic you should be able to:
- Identify the constitutional and historical factors that explain the nature of US parties.
- Identify and explain political liberalism in the USA and the main ideological views of the Democratic Party.
- Identify and explain political conservatism in the USA and the main ideological views of the Republican Party.
- Identify and explain the parties' main voting coalitions and bases of support, and any changes to these through realignments.
- Identify and explain the parties' internal divisions, giving examples of factions within each party.
- Show how and why US parties are described as organisationally weak.
- Explain the 'party decline' thesis of the 1970s.
- Explain using evidence and examples why parties are now more ideologically coherent and polarised.
- Explain using evidence and examples how parties have become organisationally stronger.
- Explain why the USA has such a strong two-party system in such a diverse nation.
- Identify and explain the difficulties facing third parties in breaking the two-party duopoly.
- Show how third parties may have some impact on the political and electoral systems despite these difficulties.
- Make relevant and appropriate references to UK parties to highlight differences.

Voting behaviour

Examiner tip

Always refer to models of voting behaviour and concepts that psephologists have developed to analyse and explain the factors influencing the way people vote.

party identification
A strong psychological/ emotional attachment to parties gained through political socialisation which leads to habit voting regardless of candidates and issues. Such party loyalty is deep-rooted and resistant to change, leading to predictable and stable voting. Such partisanship can be weak or strong and may change in response to events such as white southern voters in the 1960s.

New Deal Coalition
Voting groups attracted to the Democrats by the 1930s New Deal reforms, alongside the white conservative voters in the 'solid' South whose alignment was a legacy of the Civil War. This new coalition of liberal groups and ethnic minorities in the North supporting the same party as the extremely conservative South collapsed when the Democrats adopted more liberal and civil rights platforms in the 1960s.

Voting behaviour in the USA is regarded as considerably more complex than in other democracies because of the variables involved and the fragmented and changing electorate to which the candidates have to appeal. Psephologists have developed various models of voting behaviour to analyse the factors influencing voters. Essentially though, these come down to two basic approaches:

- **Voter profile:** a person's background (gender, age, religion, ethnicity etc.) largely explains why they vote for a particular candidate or party. There is a strong sense of **partisan alignment** and party identification. The key to winning elections therefore with this analysis is to ensure your natural supporters bother to come out and vote.
- **Recency factors:** this sees voters as more volatile, willing to change allegiance from election to election depending on factors such as the issues, the personality of the candidates and campaign advertising. This approach takes into account trends such as **partisan de-alignment**. According to this analysis, the way to electoral success is the importance of the campaign and having attractive policies to win over wavering voters.

Partisan alignment

The party identification model stresses the importance of partisanship in explaining voting behaviour. Through long-term (primacy) factors such as socioeconomic status, individuals develop strong attachments to parties and align with those parties, not changing their vote from election to election. These voters are the core voters or the base of the parties. Levels of partisanship fluctuate, but high levels lead to stable, fairly predictable patterns of voting behaviour.

Parties and their core voters

The two parties by necessity have to attract the support of diverse groups of voters, who perceive the party as representing their interests and reflecting their values. This relates to the history, ideology and policies of each party as well as to voter profile.

The Democratic Party

The Democratic Party is perceived as the more liberal party, associated with the less affluent and with minorities, and offering interventionist policies to help them. This dates back to the days of the New Deal Coalition in the 1930s. As discussed earlier it is associated with more progressive positions on issues and policies, and therefore attracts more intellectual and liberal voters to its voting coalition.

The Republican Party

The Republican Party is perceived as the more conservative party, associated with richer, WASP (White Anglo-Saxon Protestant) America, with policies favouring business, free markets and fiscal and social conservatism, and attracting more wealthy, white, rural and suburban voters to its voting coalition.

What social and economic factors influence voter choice?

Income

Although the social class factor is relatively insignificant in US political culture, there is a correlation between income levels and voting behaviour, with more affluent voters tending to vote Republican and the less affluent tending to support the Democrats. There are also occupational differences in voting: for example, unionised car workers are more likely to vote Democrat than business executives. This relates in part to the economic policies of the two parties. In 2012, Obama secured 63% of the vote of those earning under $30,000 p/a.

Race and ethnicity

The USA has always been a melting pot of immigrant groups with different cultural identities and traditions. This diversity is reflected in voting patterns according to race.

The black vote

African-Americans have been the most overwhelmingly solid group of Democrat voters since the 1930s. At this time, the black vote, which had gone mainly to the Republicans since the days of Abraham Lincoln, realigned to support the Democrats in response to the policies of Franklin Roosevelt. Usually more than 90% of black voters vote Democrat at each election (93% in 2012). The black vote is heavily concentrated in certain states and districts and in multi-ethnic cities such as Washington DC and Chicago. Although largely static in terms of overall growth as a proportion of the electorate, the growth in the black vote in Ohio from 11% (2008) to 15% (2012) certainly aided Obama's victory in this key swing state the second time around.

Why is the black vote so heavily Democratic?

Many factors pull black voters towards the Democrats and push them away from the Republicans:

- The New Deal and Great Society legacy of activist government and welfare programmes, benefiting poorer groups of voters.
- The Democratic Party's support for the Civil Rights Movement and civil rights legislation.
- The Democrats' support for, and extension of, affirmative action programmes.
- Democratic black role models, including members of Congress, governors, mayors and the first black president.
- The Republican Party's failure to support or represent black interests and its image as the white party supported by white voters.

However, a problem for black voters has been that the Republican Party ignores them because it cannot win their vote and the Democratic Party takes them for granted because it can.

Republicans have tried to attract the votes of the black middle class through economic and socially conservative policies, appealing to richer or religious black voters, but

Examiner tip

It is important to be able to identify and explain the links between each of the two US parties and the core voting coalitions that support them.

Knowledge check 27

Why is social class less significant in explaining voting behaviour in the USA than in the UK?

Knowledge check 28

Why are both US parties reluctant campaigners for the black vote?

with little success. Note though that the only African-American senator in the 2012–14 Congress is a Republican Tim Scott (SC), while others served in executive posts under George W. Bush including secretary of state Condoleezza Rice.

The Hispanic vote

The Hispanic vote is regarded as the sleeping giant of US politics as it comprises a growing proportion of the electorate. Just under 14 million Hispanics were eligible to vote in 2012, an increase of 18% on 2008. Some of the key features of the Latino vote are:

- Hispanic voters are concentrated in several key districts and states with large Electoral College votes (e.g. Florida) and so are politically significant, with their votes sought by both parties. Most are Spanish speaking and over 70% are Roman Catholic, which has led to some vote switching from the Democrats to the Republicans over issues such as abortion.
- The majority still vote Democrat for social rather than religious reasons, and in 2012 Obama won 71% of the Hispanic vote, up from 67% from 2008. Republican support for tighter immigration controls and their tougher attitude towards illegal immigrants are factors that helps explain the Democrat lead among Hispanic voters.

Knowledge check 29

Why are Hispanic voters increasingly targeted by the two parties in election campaigns?

- The growth in Florida's Hispanic electorate (17% in 2012 up from 14% in 2008) undoubtedly helped Obama in this key swing state.
- Turnout among Hispanics is, however, historically lower than for other ethnic groups, so while the challenge for the Republicans is to get them to switch their allegiance, the Democrats focus on trying to get them to turn out and vote.

The Asian vote

The Asian population represents a growing group of voters (currently 3%) and have their origins in a number of countries, including Vietnam, Japan and Korea. In the 2012 election they voted 73% Democrat and 26% Republican.

Religion

The USA is unusual in that religious identity has strongly influenced voting behaviour:

- The WASP vote was always strongly Republican because the early white settlers were Protestant.
- Catholic voters (of Irish and Italian descent as well as Hispanic) have historically identified with the Democratic Party as minorities. This has declined in recent times however, in part due to controversies over issues such as gay marriage and abortion. In 2012, Obama only narrowly won this group 50% to 48%, down 4% on 2008.
- Jewish voters are traditionally Democrat because of their minority status and liberal views, are usually active in support of pro-Israel candidates and are a key voting bloc in New York and Florida. Yet interestingly, Obama's support among them fell considerably between 2008 and 2012 from 78% to 69%, largely because of his perceived lack of unequivocal support for Israel.

Examiner tip

Be aware of the greater importance of religion and religious affiliation as a factor influencing voting behaviour in the USA compared to the UK.

- Christian fundamentalist voters are the cultural and social conservatives of US politics and strongly Republican, siding with religion in the so-called 'Culture Wars' against secular values. Romney *improved* his support among this group in 2012 securing a 78% share of their vote.

- Regular churchgoers are more likely to vote Republican, while secular voters are more likely to vote Democrat. In 2012, Obama won 62% of the vote among those who never attend religious services.

Gender

In elections, the Republican Party receives a majority of votes from men, and the Democratic Party a majority of votes from women. Recognition of the significance of the female vote was reflected in the attention given to 'security moms' in 2004 and 'hockey moms' in 2008 as important demographic groups of voters. The **gender gap** *increased* in 2012 when 55% of women voted for Obama but 52% of men backed Romney.

How can the 'gender gap' be explained?

Of course, apart from gender, all voters have other characteristics. Men and women may be rich or poor, black or white, liberal or conservative. However, the evidence suggests that women voters are more likely to vote Democrat because they:

- are more 'pro-choice' on abortion, more pro-gun control and anti-death penalty
- place more emphasis on health, education and welfare issues
- dislike much Republican social conservatism and hawkish views on foreign policy and place less emphasis on lower taxes than men
- are more environmentally aware, wanting more regulation

Age

Evidence is mixed, but there is little to show that age is a significant independent variable affecting voting behaviour. What can be said is that older voters are more likely to have a party identification and thus more likely to vote. This explains the emphasis both parties place on the 'grey vote'. Voters aged 65+ backed Romney by a margin of 56% to 44% in 2012. Younger voters are more de-aligned and volatile, and are not reliable voters, despite 'Rock the Vote' campaigns. In 2012 Obama won the votes of 60% of the 18–29-year-old voters, down from 66% in 2008.

Region

Where a voter lives in the USA can be an important influence on their voting. This relates to the different social and economic characteristics of the states and areas within them. The southern states were solidly Democratic until the 1960s and have been solidly Republican since then. Voters in the rust belt, the industrial states, the coastal states and the cities ('blue America') are more likely to vote Democrat, and voters in the Bible belt, the mountain states and the rural and suburban areas within them are more likely to vote Republican ('red America').

US voters, therefore, have different group identifications and interests that influence the way they vote. If these reinforce one another (cross-cutting identifications), it is easier to predict voting behaviour. For example, a high-income, white, male, Protestant executive living in a Texas suburb is likely to be a reliable Republican voter, while a low-income, female, atheist, black waitress living in an inner city in New Jersey is likely to be a Democrat voter.

gender gap This refers to the different voting patterns of men and women found in all modern elections, although the gap narrows or widens at each election as voters respond to different candidates and issues. Women voters are more likely to vote Democrat and men Republican. This links to the ideologies and policies of both parties being more or less attractive to the different genders.

Knowledge check 30

Why do parties focus on the 'grey vote' in US elections?

Knowledge check 31

Give two examples of voters with 'cross-cutting identifications'.

Examiner tip

Always use accurate statistical evidence from recent elections showing links between groups of voters with differing social and demographic characteristics and their support for the parties. Figures for the 2012 election are cited frequently in this guide, so learn some of the key ones.

swing voters Labelled floating in the UK and independent in the USA, swing voters are de-aligned and lack strong party identification, and their votes cannot be predicted or taken for granted. They are targeted in campaigns and can be crucial in deciding elections, especially in swing states. Approximately 30% of voters describe themselves as independent, although most 'lean' towards one party or another.

Partisan de-alignment

An alternative model of voting behaviour stresses the increasing importance of short-term factors in explaining voting behaviour.

In recent times this has been put down largely to increased de-alignment. Its consequences include: more volatility, a greater likelihood of ticket-splitting, and an increased numbers of swing voters. It also means that parties must work harder to win votes, especially independents, as they can no longer rely on large numbers of core, aligned voters to always turn out and vote for them.

However, there are debates about the extent of de-alignment in the USA. Paradoxically, ticket-splitting has declined in recent elections and there are fewer 'swing states' or competitive House districts. What matters most is understanding what form these short-term factors can take.

What are short-term (recency) factors influencing voting?

Candidate voting

De-aligned voters may vote differently in different elections because their voting is more influenced by the candidates (their personality, image, experience) than by their party allegiance. This is particularly the case in the age of media-dominated politics focusing on candidate-centred campaigns. Reagan in the 1980s was fêted as the 'Great Communicator'. McCain may have been seen as too old and 'grumpy' in 2008 and Obama as the more impressive candidate. In 2012, Romney did himself no favours by committing several gaffes caught on camera, such as implying he did not care about the 47% of the population he claimed were dependent on government support.

Issue voting

De-aligned voters are also more likely to vote for candidates because of their views on specific issues, particularly in the age of single-issue politics, with economic issues usually being the most significant.

Knowledge check 32

Which issues were 'salient' at (a) the 2004 election, (b) the 2012 election?

However, election issues change, and in 2004 it was said not to be 'the economy, stupid' (as in Clinton's 1992 campaign) but moral values that were uppermost when 'wedge issues' such as abortion and gay marriage were used to energise the base of the Republican Party to vote. By 2012 in the wake of the financial crisis and bank bail-outs, the economy was again centre stage, with 59% voters saying it was the most important issue compared to just 5% for foreign policy. It was also a chance to deliver a verdict on Obama's first term. Some commentators summed up his main achievements as, 'Bin Laden's dead and General Motors is alive.'

Performance voting

Examiner tip

No two elections are the same. Be prepared to give evidence of different candidates, issues and events in several presidential elections producing different outcomes.

According to rational choice theories of voting behaviour, voters may vote on the performance or record of an incumbent or a future president. Retrospective voting suggests voters make judgements on past performance and vote against politicians with a poor performance in office, as in the case of Bush Senior in 1992 after recession, or they make a judgement on prospective performance, as with Obama in 2008. When voters are satisfied with his performance, the incumbent may be elected to a second term, as were Clinton in 1996 (economic boom) and George W. Bush in 2004 (war president). Arguably Obama was re-elected in 2012 not so much because voters were satisfied with the record of his first term, but because of the flaws of his opponent.

The October surprise

This is the term given to an unexpected event close to election day where the side disadvantaged by it does not have time to respond properly. In 2008 it was the revelation that Obama had a half-aunt living in the US as an illegal immigrant. In 2012 it was Hurricane Sandy to which the president was felt to have responded effectively, even earning praise from the high-profile Republican governor of New Jersey, Chris Christie. By dominating the headlines for several days, it took the momentum out of Romney's campaign and showed Obama in a positive presidential light. The October surprise rarely changes the final result, but can make life easier or harder respectively for the candidates in the final days of campaigning.

What is 'split-ticket' voting?

Because of the separation of powers and federalism, US voters face a choice from a range of candidates, for several offices, on the same ballot paper on the same day. Voters can vote the 'straight ticket' by voting for the same party for each office. Voters who vote for candidates for office from different parties on the same ballot paper at the same election are 'splitting their ticket'. The simplest reason why voters do this (although it may seem irrational) is because they can. Other reasons include voter de-alignment and the influence of different candidates and issues, so voters are making complex choices by voting for different parties for different reasons.

Split-ticket voting was high in the 1970s and 1980s, and in 1984 55% of Democratic identifiers voted for Reagan, but he was faced with a Democrat majority in the House. However, split-ticket voting has fluctuated and declined overall in recent elections.

Consequences of split-ticket voting

- It can lead to divided government in Washington, and the much-criticised legislative 'gridlock' when laws and policies are difficult to get passed.
- Arguably, it offers a better deal for voters who may get the best of both worlds through their votes: for example, voting for a Republican president can mean low taxes but strong defence and voting for a Democrat member of Congress can mean higher spending on welfare.
- It helps to prevent an 'elective dictatorship', since the voters' choices result in more effective checks and balances.

Abstention in US elections

Surprisingly for the self-declared beacon of democracy, the US has one of the lowest turnouts for elections in the Western world. It reached its lowest point in 1996 when turnout was barely over 50% of eligible voters (not all eligible voters choose to register to vote), though it has increased in subsequent elections. It rose in 2008 to just under 62%, before dropping back to around 58% in 2012. Turnout fell in all but two states in 2012 (Iowa and Louisiana). Turnout in some primaries can be even lower: only 5% of eligible voters in Virginia's Republican primary in March 2012 bothered to turn out to vote.

de-alignment This term refers to the lack or loss of party identification, so it links with the concept of independent swing voters. De-aligned voters lack or lose partisan loyalty gained through socialisation into party identification from an early age. De-alignment links with volatility, split-ticket voting and higher abstention, as well as candidate and issue voting. Younger voters are more de-aligned than older voters.

split-ticket voting Federalism and the separation of powers enable voters to vote for different parties on the same ballot in the same election on the same day. Voters who vote for different parties for whatever reason (candidates/issues) are voting a split rather than a straight party ticket, and can be seen by examining voting statistics in states showing different levels of support for different candidates from the same party.

Knowledge check 33

How accurate is it to see turnout in US elections as continually falling?

Federalism and the separation of powers mean that there are numerous elections at different levels of government and for different offices as well as primaries and direct democracy. Americans vote 'for the president to the local dog-catcher' in 80,000 units of government, leading to 'permanent' campaigns and 'bed-sheet ballots' which may lead to voter fatigue, higher alienation levels and abstention through too many participation opportunities.

The causes of relatively high US abstention levels are explained by multiple factors relating to the electoral and political systems. It is never enough to state that voters are simply 'bored' or 'apathetic' or 'cynical'. Boredom, apathy or cynicism must be explained.

Why does turnout fluctuate in presidential elections?

How can high abstention be explained?

Voter registration

In most states, voters have to make some effort to get registered, but it is now easier, as the Help America Vote Act (HAVA) 2002 allows same-day registration and early voting in many states. There are registration drives to mobilise the vote and there are no legal barriers to voting (except for felony in some states) following civil rights amendments in the 1960s. Despite this, many voters fail to register. The registration process therefore helps explain why fewer eligible Americans might choose to register to vote (it takes a little bit of effort) but does not really explain why many who registered still do not turn out and exercise their democratic and constitutional right to choose their leaders.

'Democratic overload' and 'voter fatigue'

The huge number of elections for a wide range of posts from the president down to local civic officials and the resulting sense of permanent campaigning cause voters to switch off.

Media-dominated campaigns

The politics of sound bites, photo opportunities and negative advertising, with candidates spending millions of dollars to say little about real issues, can alienate voters.

The electoral system/lack of choice

It has been argued that the first-past-the-post electoral system discourages third party and independent candidates, leaving voters with little real choice. As both parties need to appeal to the centre, the choice is often seen as between bland and blander. The Electoral College system increases this sense of the 'wasted vote' syndrome. Voters in 'safe' states might see little point in voting, as their vote will not have any effect on the overall result.

Decline in partisanship

Voters with strong party identification use their vote, while those without tend not to. The growth of party de-alignment helps explain declining turnout since the 1960s.

Voter apathy and cynicism

Some voters feel that voting does not make any difference to their lives, and that remote, lobbyist-dominated government in Washington is not responsive to their views. Cynicism has been increased by dissatisfaction with presidential performance and political scandals.

'Hapathy'

The idea that voters are so content that they do not need to vote is known as 'hapathy'. In this view, it is satisfaction with the system, not alienation from it that reduces turnout. This, however, can hardly be said to apply to the 2012 election when the majority of voters identified the economy as the most important issue facing America.

Differential abstention

Although turnout overall is low in the US for reasons identified above, we must also be aware that some groups are more likely to vote than others, and may not vote in every election. This is known as **differential abstention**. Low-income, less-educated, younger and Hispanic voters are more likely to abstain, which damages the Democrats' prospects. Abstention is lower among high-income, elderly, educated, suburban white voters, which helps the Republican cause.

Turnout is lower in the mid-terms, where incumbency may be a strong factor influencing outcomes, and is even lower for primary elections.

By contrast, turnout can rise if:

- The state is a 'battleground' state. Turnout was high, for example, in North Carolina in 2012 at over 64%. By contrast, the lowest turnout (44%) then was in Hawaii, a strongly 'blue state'.
- There are other high profile issues or election contests on the ballot too. The highest turnout of any state in 2012 was in Minnesota, which also had an initiative measure to ban gay marriage on the ballot.

Some comparisons with the UK

Voting behaviour in the UK (in comparison with the USA) is characterised by:

- easy and compulsory registration of voters
- higher turnouts (65% in 2010)
- the requirement for the voter to mark the ballot paper with a single cross: ticket splitting is not possible
- fewer voting opportunities
- the role of class as the single most important determinant of the vote
- less emphasis on religious or ethnic factors influencing voting behaviour

differential abstention
Voters vote or abstain differently at each election, which may be won or lost according to which voters turn out to vote and which do not. Large numbers of young and minority voters voted for Obama in 2008, but failed to vote in the 2010 mid-term elections, while many Republican voters who abstained in 2008 voted in the 2010 mid-terms, giving the Republican Party success.

Examiner tip

Statistical and demographic information relating to US voting behaviour can be obtained through the Pew Research Center (**www. pewresearch.org**) and the US Census Bureau (**www.census.gov**).

After studying this topic you should be able to:

- Understand and use key psephological concepts and models of voting behaviour.
- Understand and explain the broad voting coalitions supporting each of the two parties, their core voting support and any changes that have taken place to these.
- Know that the outcomes of US elections are affected by a mixture of long-term and short-term factors influencing the way voters vote and that these are different at each election.
- Understand and explain the links between the social characteristics of US voters (socioeconomic status, gender, religion, race and ethnicity, age and region) and their support for the parties.
- Explain the importance of recency factors affecting the outcome of each election, such as different candidates, issues and events influencing voting behaviour.
- Understand the causes and the consequences of split-ticket voting in US elections.
- Understand the causes and consequences of differing levels of abstention at each US election.
- Make comparisons with voting in the UK where relevant and appropriate.
- Recognise the key debates and competing arguments in the study of US voting behaviour.

Summary

Pressure groups

What is a pressure group?

Pressure groups are organised groups who share a common interest that they wish to protect or a common aim that they wish to promote. They seek to influence policy by gaining access to decision makers who have power. Therefore, compared to parties, pressure groups represent narrower interests and have narrower aims, do not put up candidates in elections and do not seek or take responsibility for government.

Pressure groups are found in a pluralist democracy where citizens can form or join groups to express their very diverse views and interests to government. **Pluralist** theory is associated with the political scientist Robert Dahl, who argued that governments respond to citizens' views expressed through competing pressure groups which all have the potential to influence decision making.

Pluralists take a positive view of pressure groups and argue that as a result of their activities political power is dispersed within the political system, although they do not consider that all pressure groups have an equal influence on government. Pluralists argue that groups are only influential in narrow policy areas: for instance, the American Medical Association (AMA) has influence on health policy but not on foreign policy. Also, on most issues there are *countervailing groups*: for example, 'pro-choice' groups promote a different agenda from 'pro-life' groups.

This pluralist view of pressure groups, however, is challenged by proponents of **elite theory**, who argue that power is not dispersed but is in fact highly concentrated, with some groups much more powerfully organised and well-funded to influence the political agenda. They argue that there is not a level playing field when it comes to influence over political decisions.

Irrespective of the variations in power that they possess, there are a wide range of pressure groups in the US representing sections of society and issues from across the whole political spectrum.

What are the main types of pressure group in the USA?

Economic pressure groups

Business groups can gain access to, and influence over, economic decision making and include multinational corporations such as Microsoft, and 'peak' associations speaking for the business community, such as the US Chamber of Commerce. Labour groups are trade unions which are active on issues affecting their members' interests. The 'peak' association speaking for this sector is the AFL/CIO, which lobbies on behalf of organised labour. It usually supports the Democratic Party, providing funds and campaign workers. Professional associations are 'protective' groups organised to defend specific occupational interests, such as the AMA, which represents US doctors and has been active in opposing attempts to expand universal healthcare.

AQA A2 Government & Politics

Single-issue lobbies

In recent years there has been a huge growth in the number of groups representing single issues and specific causes. Examples include 'pro-choice' and 'pro-life' groups on the issue of abortion, and Freedom to Marry, which promotes same sex marriage.

Public interest lobbies

Consumer groups and citizens' lobbies, seeking a more collective good, have grown as new public interest issues and 'causes' have surfaced, such as the Sierra Club, an environmental group lobbying on environmental issues, and the American Civil Liberties Union (ACLU), formed to promote and protect citizens' liberties. Common Cause, a public interest group, puts the case for consumer rights and has battled against the corporate oil and tobacco lobbies in the USA.

Why has activity grown in recent years?

- The growth of government intervention in health, welfare and the environment means that government regulates large areas of citizens' lives, so groups are formed to defend their interests vis-à-vis government.
- A highly specialised and socially diverse society like the USA has thousands of different occupations and views on issues, with groups forming to protect and promote these.
- The complexity of modern government decision making means that lobbying is needed to provide specialised information to decision makers.
- One of the shortcomings of representative democracy expressed through voting at elections is that a 'blanket vote' for party candidates means citizens cannot express their specific views and interests.
- The opportunity in many states for ballot initiatives on highly-charged single issue topics, such as legalising marijuana and changing state abortion laws, often involve the relevant pressure groups heavily in campaigning.

It is said that the growing number of lobbies operating in US politics leads to a state of 'hyper-pluralism', in which government is overloaded with demands from powerful groups.

How do pressure groups achieve their aims?

Pressure groups in the USA use different methods at different times:
- Direct action, such as demonstrations, sit-ins or violence — normally favoured by *outsider* groups, such as the Occupy movement.
- Making effective use of the many access points in the States, such as Congress and the Supreme Court.
- Direct lobbying of the government or Congress — generally favoured by *insider* groups who are well funded and normally have good contacts in Washington, such as the NRA.
- Bringing and funding court cases to the Supreme Court.
- Encouraging their members to write directly to their senator or congressman.
- Publicity: broadcasting television ads or mailing out leaflets.

Examiner tip

Make sure you have several examples of different kinds of US pressure group, with evidence of their differing aims, protective or promotional, and their specific activities to achieve those aims.

Knowledge check 36

Explain, using examples, what is meant by a single-issue pressure group.

Examiner tip

Know the reasons why pressure group activity has become so widespread in the USA and how the US political culture encourages and enhances such activity.

- Endorsing favoured candidates at election time, often by producing candidate score cards so that electors can see the voting record/public stance of the various candidates. The NRA grades candidates, and securing their top A* endorsement can prove very important electorally in certain states such as Ohio.

Access points in the political system

This relates to the points where pressure groups can gain access to government in order to influence decisions. The US system of government is fragmented, open and multi-access. It is important to note that a group cannot influence anyone until it has access to them and their decision making.

The legislative branch

The House of Representatives and the Senate are equally powerful houses. Party allegiance has a relatively weak influence on the way members of Congress vote, so both houses are open to influence from pressure groups, especially if the group in question helped fund a member's campaign. Because Congress has a fragmented power structure of committees and sub-committees, some pressure groups can gain access here, where they focus on lobbying on the detail of legislation passing through both houses.

The executive branch

This branch of government may be lobbied via the Executive Office of the President (EXOP) or through access to federal government departments and agencies where policy or legislation originates or is implemented. The president also has the power of veto over legislation, and pressure groups may lobby for this to be used if they have failed to halt a bill they dislike in either house of Congress.

The judicial branch

The Supreme Court makes crucial decisions on controversial issues, so some pressure groups try to exert influence here:
- The NAACP uses the Supreme Court to challenge segregation by providing amicus curiae (friend of the court) briefs to influence its decisions and the NRA was involved in the landmark case *DC* v *Heller* in 2009, supporting 2nd Amendment rights.
- The American Civil Liberties Union (ACLU) brings test cases before the court, dealing with issues such as imprisonment without trial in Guantánamo Bay.
- Pressure groups may try to influence presidential selection of Supreme Court justices when a vacancy arises, or in Senate confirmation hearings.

This federal separation of powers is mirrored at the state level of government. Many decisions affecting groups are made at the state level, so pressure groups lobby here, for example, influencing state laws relating to abortion and its accessibility.

What are the most important factors affecting the success of pressure groups?

To succeed in gaining access to decision makers, pressure groups need a range of resources. These will vary, but they include the following:

Knowledge check 37

Why and how is the Supreme Court used as an access point by some pressure groups?

Membership

- A large membership is especially important when supporters of the pressure group are likely to vote. The American Association of Retired People (AARP), for example, speaks on behalf of 40 million members.
- A smaller but powerful and active membership can also be very effective, such as the National Rifle Association (NRA), with over 4 million members.
- A dispersed membership can make up an important voting bloc in all the states: this is true, for example, of veterans' organisations.

Money

Groups raise money to try to gain access to elected politicians through financial contributions to their campaigns, either through political action committee money (see later) or by 'spending on behalf of' candidates, buying advertising to promote issues that may help their favoured candidates to win.

Professional lobbyists

Wealthy pressure groups hire professional lobbyists to make links with members of Congress in order to try to influence their voting in committees where the details of legislation are worked out. Especially important are former members of Congress, who may pass through the 'revolving door', widely perceived as linking service in Congress with jobs in the lobbying sector, and be hired by groups wishing to use their expert knowledge of Capitol Hill and their contacts there to influence decisions.

Information and expertise

Because the majority of political issues are now highly complex and technical, some pressure groups will gain access to congressional decision making because they have the specialist knowledge needed to testify in congressional hearings.

Other factors

- Groups are more influential when united in their aims, and weaker when they are internally divided. For example, there is no single pro-gun control group to meet the political firepower of the NRA.
- Groups are more effective when they are concerned with narrow policy aims or issues accepted by public opinion as realistic and worth supporting.
- Groups are more effective when they are inside government decision making. The strong relationship between powerful groups and government (known as 'clientelism') is referred to as an iron triangle, linking a pressure group, a federal government department or agency and the relevant congressional committee in a relationship which is hard to break or regulate.

What 'outsider' strategies are pursued by US pressure groups?

Many pressure groups in the USA lack the resources described above, and so fail to gain access. Others do not wish to pursue an insider strategy. In both cases, they use different methods of influence to achieve their aims:

Knowledge check 38

How and why do pressure groups support candidates at elections?

lobbying Attempting to influence policy decisions by gaining access to legislators and bureaucrats in order to initiate, pass, amend or defeat legislation. It involves professional lobbyists in lobbying firms contacting government officials and testifying at congressional committee hearings, which often rely on lobbyists for expert advice.

Knowledge check 39

What is the 'revolving door' and why is it criticised?

iron triangle The term denoting a three-sided, mutually supportive, stable relationship between the congressional committees (which fund and oversee programmes), a federal department or agency (which regulates them) and a special interest group (which benefits from them). The triangle dominates policy making in that area in their mutual interests (sometimes called a sub-government), such as the military–industrial complex or agriculture or veterans iron triangles.

- **Public campaigns.** Groups try to influence public opinion through the media in order to exert an indirect influence on politicians, in the knowledge that most politicians pay attention to the views of 'the folks back home' in their districts and states, particularly near election time.
- **Grass-roots lobbying and mass mailing campaigns.** These have become more important as electronic technology progresses, allowing groups to mobilise supporters to swamp their representatives with e-mail or letters in an attempt to influence their votes. They may publish ratings on voting records relating to the group's aims.
- **Direct action and demonstrations.** Because of 1st Amendment rights, taking to the streets as a form of protest is common in the USA. The aim is to draw media, public and congressional attention to the group and its aims, to raise public awareness and show strength of feeling on the issue. Examples include the Civil Rights campaigns of the 1950s and 1960s, anti-war demonstrations, the Million Mom March in 2000 over guns and the Occupy Wall Street anti-capitalist protest of 2011.
- **The initiative process.** Grass-roots activity is particularly important in states that allow initiatives. Pressure groups raise signatures to initiate a proposition on the ballot paper supporting their aims. They then campaign for this to be passed at state level.

Some pressure groups are very successful in achieving their aims and others are not. Some get what they want most of the time, but others do not. It all depends on variables.

Are pressure groups a threat to democracy?

Those who believe that pressure groups are inevitable in a liberal, pluralist democracy and beneficial to it argue that they are *not* a threat to democracy:
- Pressure groups are the voice of the people, representing specific views and interests not catered for by catch-all parties and 'blanket votes' at elections.
- They encourage citizens' participation and involvement in politics.
- They link citizens and government between elections, keeping governments aware of different views on issues.
- The competing views of pressure groups help governments to decide where the public interest lies on issues such as environmental protection.
- Pressure group balance means that on most issues there are competing voices, such as business and labour.
- Groups play a valuable role in governmental decision making, in that they provide the expertise, cooperation and consent needed if policy is to work.

Others believe that pressure groups are too powerful and hinder the workings of a liberal democracy, and thus *are* a threat to it:
- There is unequal representation of interests, with many groups lacking access to the corridors of power or the resources to acquire it.
- Some interest groups are unorganised or ineffectively organised (e.g. the poor, who can be ignored), while others are powerfully organised (e.g. corporate lobbies such as energy companies or professional bodies).
- Some single-issue groups threaten the democratic process by blocking reforms in areas such as gun law reform (NRA) or environmental regulation (oil and energy lobbies) which are wanted by a majority of the population.

direct action Groups with little or no access to decision makers may use 'outsider' strategies to influence them indirectly by gaining media and public attention. Direct action may be violent or illegal, such as actions to close down abortion clinics, or non-violent, such as demonstrations and forms of civil disobedience seen during the Civil Rights Movement. This may reflect weakness rather than strength.

Examiner tip

Different pressure groups use different methods at different times and with different degrees of success, so make sure you can give examples of these variables and be careful not to over-generalise when analysing their activities.

- Budget deficits are linked to strong lobbies pressing for more resources and too strong to be denied by members of Congress seeking re-election.
- There is criticism of methods used by some groups, such as the role of political action committees in electoral finance or 'pro-life' groups harassing workers in abortion clinics.

Are there checks to pressure group power?

- The number of access points means groups may get what they want in the House but not in the Senate, or may achieve their aims at federal but not state level. Access does not mean success.
- The variety of pressure groups and countervailing groups creates a degree of balance.
- The Federal Election Campaign Act (FECA) places restrictions on political action committees' funding of candidates that must be disclosed.
- The mass media, protected by 1st Amendment rights, may uncover lobbying scandals, such as the Jack Abramoff 'influence peddling' case in 2006.
- Public opinion can restrain pressure group power, as members of Congress listen to 'the folks back home' even when being swamped by an artificially manufactured 'astro-turf' pressure group mail campaign.
- Legal restrictions on lobbying make it illegal to offer bribes to members of Congress, and all lobbyists must register as such, making their activities open and transparent.
- The Honest Leadership and Open Government Act of 2007, passed as a result of the Abramoff case, led to the tightening of regulations on lobbying activities such as a 2-year 'cooling off' period and the banning of gifts and sponsored trips for members of Congress.

The answer to the question of whether pressure groups are too powerful is 'It depends.' No pressure group is all-powerful.

Political action committees

Political action committees (PACs) are the financial arms of pressure groups, set up to raise campaign funds and channel them to support or oppose candidates in electoral contests. They grew after the FECA reforms of the 1970s restricted fund-raising from organisations and 'fat cats', leaving a funding gap to be filled. They are limited in the amount of hard money they can donate to candidates ($5,000), but they 'bundle' these contributions to increase the sum given. They also give money for 'issue advocacy' to advertise 'on behalf of' candidates. Most PACs are pragmatic in their support, donating to candidates from both parties who will win, which generally means incumbents rather than challengers. This helps them achieve access to decision makers, especially the chairs and members of congressional committees affecting their interests. The role of PACs is controversial, with debates over their effect on US politics:

- Their impact on the electoral process, with millions of dollars raised and spent by groups, can be vital in a close race. Some argue that members of Congress will not speak out against powerful interests (e.g. the NRA or the pro-Israel lobby) because they are afraid of being targeted for defeat.

Examiner tip
There are debates, but no agreement, on whether pressure groups enhance democracy or hinder it, so be aware of the arguments used on both sides of the analysis.

Examiner tip
Do not underestimate the significance of checks to pressure group power and the constraints on their activities in a democracy. The Centre for Responsive Politics website (**www. opensecrets.org**) tracks pressure group activities and funding.

- They bolster the rise of candidate-centred campaigns, as they support candidates, not parties. Elected candidates then feel more beholden to them than to their parties, which can affect how they vote in Congress.
- They encourage influence peddling in a 'coin-operated Congress' where it is alleged you 'have to pay to play'.
- They can deter challengers to incumbent members of Congress.
- New Super PACS emerged after the *FEC* v *Citizens United* case in 2010, allowing the unlimited raising and spending of campaign funds as long as they do not coordinate their activities with the parties or candidates (see p. 17).

Knowledge check 40

Why are political action committees and their activities often criticised?

Comparisons with UK pressure groups

- The UK offers fewer access points, as it has a fusion of power and a unitary system.
- There are fewer checks and balances in the UK, so less opportunity for groups to influence and block legislation.
- The UK has a strong party system, so MPs are protected from group influence by a strong party line.
- UK candidates are funded by the parties, not pressure groups with PACs.
- There are no entrenched rights and less open government in the UK, so group activity is less effective.
- There are fewer opportunities for US-style groups to operate in the UK, with no primaries and no initiatives.
- There is a clearer distinction in the UK between 'insider' groups that have access to Whitehall and 'outsider' groups that do not.

Summary

After studying this topic you should be able to:
- Define pressure groups and show how and why they arise in a representative democracy.
- Show that there are different theoretical perspectives on the role of pressure groups in a representative democracy.
- Give examples of different types of pressure group operating in the US political system.
- Show why pressure groups and their activities have grown in recent years and why US political culture encourages this activity.
- Give examples of the variables that affect the methods that pressure groups use to try and achieve their aims and objectives.
- Explain the different access points that pressure groups may use to further their specific aims and why different groups may use different access points at different times.
- Explain the reasons why some pressure groups may be more successful than others in achieving their aims.

- Explain, using examples, why some pressure groups may resort to 'outsider' strategies to try and achieve their aims.
- Evaluate the ways in which pressure group activity may enhance representative democracy.
- Evaluate the criticisms made of some pressure group activities and methods that may serve to hinder the workings of representative democracy.
- Know of the several checks to pressure group power in the USA, including legislative ones, and that not all groups are all-powerful all of the time.
- Evaluate the causes and the consequences of the growth of political action committees in campaign finance.
- Make comparisons where relevant and necessary to the relatively weaker pressure groups that operate in the UK political system.
- Recognise the key debates and competing arguments on the role and influence of pressure groups in the US political system.

Questions & Answers

This section looks at answers to examination questions on Unit 3A and follows the four areas previously identified in the specification.

The unit test explained

The Unit 3A exam is 90 minutes in length and you must answer two questions from a choice of four. The questions will reflect the four parts of the unit.

Each of the four questions has two parts:
- Part (a) is worth 10 marks and is a short-answer question. This should be completed in around 8–10 minutes. If you spend more time on this, you will eat into the time needed to complete the more mark-rich and challenging essays.
- Part (b) is worth 30 marks and is an extended essay. At least 30–35 minutes should be spent on each of the two essays chosen.

The two parts will be connected in the sense that they are part of the same topic area being assessed. They are not necessarily connected in any other way, to prevent any possible overlap in the answers given to both questions.

Assessment objectives at A2

Although the three assessment objectives at A2 are the same as at AS, they are weighted differently. At A2 more marks are awarded for analysis (AO2) than for knowledge (AO1).

AO1: Demonstrate knowledge and understanding of relevant institutions, processes, political concepts, theories and debates.

AO2: Analyse and evaluate political information, arguments and explanations, and identify parallels, connections, similarities and differences between aspects of the political systems studied.

AO3: Construct and communicate coherent arguments, making use of a range of appropriate political vocabulary.

When you write your answer both to part (a) and part (b), you will be given marks for all three of these assessment objectives. These will be totalled to give the mark for each part of the question, with a maximum score of 40 (10 + 30) for each question. The total mark for the unit is 80. This means that the total mark can be achieved in a variety of ways, and students may show different strengths or weaknesses in their answers. Generally, a very good student will achieve high marks on all three assessment objectives, as the answer will demonstrate high levels of knowledge and understanding and excellent analytical skills, will have structure and coherence, and will include impressive political vocabulary. However, it is possible to gain high marks for one objective and lower marks for another. For example, a student's knowledge of a topic may be impressive but the answer may lack focus and analysis and it may not be very clearly communicated. This

means the mark may be high on AO1 but lower on AO2 and AO3. You should be aware of these assessment objectives and practise them throughout the year in homework essays and timed essays in class.

Levels of response

A2 assessment uses a generic mark scheme including levels of response, which examiners follow in order to allocate marks to students' answers. There is also a separate mark scheme for each specific question, reflecting the content expected in the answer.

- Level 4 is the highest level of response. Students who achieve marks at the top of this level will have written answers which are comprehensive, fully address the requirements of the question, give clear and accurate evidence and excellent examples and include developed theories and concepts, communicating clearly and effectively with focus, direction and conclusions. These are high A students.
- Level 3 responses are 'good' rather than 'excellent'. Students 'clearly' rather than 'comprehensively' address the requirements of the question and give 'good' evidence and examples, communicated 'well'.
- Level 2 responses are characterised by the key word 'limited', where students show limited knowledge, with a limited attempt to address the requirements of the question, limited evidence, examples and concepts, and communication which is limited in clarity, vocabulary, focus and direction.
- Level 1 responses should be avoided at all costs. At the bottom of this level it is barely worth entering the examination room. The key word here is 'little': the student shows little in terms of knowledge, focus, evidence, examples and clear communication. These responses are usually simplistic or superficial narrative with little clarity.

On the following pages, each sample question is accompanied by two answers written under timed conditions. One is of A-grade standard and the other of C-grade standard. None of the answers should be regarded as a perfect response. Each answer featured here only represents a way of approaching the question set, followed by an indication of the grade that it is likely to achieve and why.

After each of the questions, there is a section indicated by ⊜ identifying the focus of the question and what is expected in the answer. Each answer is followed by an 'examiner's comment' indicated by the symbol ⊜: this section comments on the approach of the answer and explains some of the reasons why it has achieved the grade indicated or how a higher mark could have been achieved. If you read these sections carefully, you will get an idea of how to improve your mark in the real examination for both parts of the question. It will also help you become more familiar with the assessment objectives.

It would be good practice to attempt your own answers *before* looking at the student answers and the comments made, so that you can do your own comparisons and make any adjustments likely to increase your mark.

It is important to note that this section does not offer any 'model answers' that can be reproduced in an examination. Most examination questions are worded differently, even when they are in the same specification area, and it is possible to achieve exactly the same grade for a question in different ways, by scoring on the assessment objectives with different strengths, weaknesses, evidence and examples. At A2, remember that not just knowledge and description (AO1) but also the higher-level skills of analysis and evaluation (AO2) are especially important if you are to gain higher marks.

How to achieve top grades

- Make sure you have covered all the specification topics in your revision to extend your question choice and to understand links between the four areas of GOV 3A.
- Consult mark schemes and assessment objectives to understand how examiners will mark your answers.
- Answer the question that has been set, not the one you wish had been set.
- Analyse the question. Identify key words in the question and refer to them in your answer where possible. Make a short plan that will guide your answer.
- Always keep a tight focus on the question asked, in the introduction, in the middle and at the end. Don't drift from its key demands.
- Use up-to-date examples and evidence to back up your arguments at all times.
- Show contextual awareness and understanding of the topic wherever possible.
- Use political concepts, theories and vocabulary, quoting political scientists or political thinkers if possible.
- Avoid learnt model answers based on questions set in previous papers.
- Use your time well: don't repeat points already made, and don't conclude your answer by simply repeating all you have said before.
- Avoid simplistic assertions and sweeping generalisations in your answers. Don't give your personal opinions or use the word 'I'.
- Be aware of debates surrounding political topics. The answer to many political questions is 'It depends', and valid (although not necessarily equal) arguments can be identified on both sides of any political debate.
- Make sure you use a good writing style, usually determined by lots of essay-writing practice throughout the year. Write with clarity and direction, with good grammar, vocabulary, spelling and legibility, to make a good overall impression on the examiner, who is going to give you a mark for your communication skills. Essays that gain high marks will have a good introduction setting the essay in context, well-developed and convincing arguments backed up by evidence and examples wherever possible, and a conclusion that draws the threads together. Lack of coherence substantially reduces marks.
- Although there are times when a passing reference to your UK politics course will be relevant to demonstrate synoptic understanding, especially of differences between the politics of the two countries, do not feel that artificial UK references have to be added to every point made or simply add on a reference to the UK at the end of the essay almost as an afterthought. Synoptic understanding demonstrates understanding of the A-level course as a whole, not just its parts, and the links both within and between the modules.
- Students who enter the examination room unprepared and lacking in serious study, and whose answers are unfocused, confused and poorly written, with little evidence of knowledge, understanding and analytical and communication skills, are unlikely to achieve the grade they wish for — but they may get the grade they deserve.

Question 1 **Electoral process and direct democracy**

(a) Explain the significance of ballot initiatives in US politics (10 marks)

e When answering this question it is essential to focus on the importance of ballot initiatives and not just on describing what they are. You should also cite one or two recent examples (AO1) and above all, evaluate their importance compared say to federal elections, and the limits to their impact (AO2). There is also some scope to consider the good and bad points of them as well, again to demonstrate AO2.

> **A-grade answer**

(a) Ballot initiatives often called propositions, are quite significant in US politics. However, they do have limits and arguably other aspects such as congressional and presidential elections are more important **a**. They can be viewed as important as they enable voters to participate directly in making laws and political decisions rather than relying on their elected representatives. Voters can initiate ballots on a wide range of issues such as gay marriage, local taxes and even legalising marijuana **b**. They therefore encourage at least in theory, voter participation and political engagement/debate. However, their significance is hindered by several factors. Firstly not all states have them **b** — the most notable that does is California **a**. Also the measures only apply to individual states; there is no scope in the US for a national ballot initiative. Some have argued that they are a poor way of deciding complex issues and have also questioned how far they represent the views of ordinary Americans. Many ballots are initiated by powerful interest and pressure groups that also spend large amounts on campaigning so are not really as 'grassroots' a form of democracy as is often claimed **a**.

The results of initiatives are also not completely binding, and can be overturned by the courts (state and federal) if they break the constitution. This happened for example in 2013 when Prop 8 was struck down in the Supreme Court **a**. Some have also argued that initiatives lead to 'voter fatigue' **c**, especially when there are a large number of initiatives on a ballot. Although the most significant form (compared to recall elections and referendums **c**) of direct democracy in the US, arguably initiatives are less important than national elections and the courts because their outcomes are not always binding and can often lead to more problems than they solve **b**.

e This candidate has handled the question impressively, demonstrating in several places **a** good knowledge and understanding of ballot initiatives and their impact (AO1) including one recent example. The answer also clearly focuses on the question, which is about significance and does not merely describe. There is some convincing analysis too **b** in several places (AO2) including not just the more obvious criticisms, but also comparing them alongside other aspects of the electoral system and the legal challenges they can face. These unexpected but perceptive comments put the answer at the top of the marks scale. There is also some use of specialist political vocabulary **c**, and generally the answer is well written and clearly structured, which gains marks for AO3. There could perhaps be a little more development of criticisms of direct democracy being the 'device of despots', but with the limited time available that does not detract from the overall quality of the answer.

C-grade answer

(a) Ballot initiatives are a form of direct democracy and are common in the USA **d**. They allow people to decide on issues that they really care about which their representatives in Congress may not **e**. Initiatives come from below not above in contrast to referendums. Ballot initiatives are especially popular in California where Prop 13 in 1978 reduced taxes **a**. Many valid criticisms have been made of them however. For instance, some say they give the majority the power to discriminate against minorities such as gays and immigrants **b**. Also a lot of money is spent in campaigning over the issues by pressure groups, churches etc. and this switches a lot of people off voting because they dislike all the TV ads and negative campaigning that can occur. They also only affect the individual state such as California and not the whole of the USA. However, they are popular with many Americans so are significant because they are a different and additional form of democracy compared with normal elections for the White House and Congress **c**.

(e) This candidate clearly has some understanding of initiatives and there are relevant examples, however these are either rather old **a** or a bit vague **b**. It would have been helpful if the candidate had explained more precisely about gay marriage and referred directly to Prop 8, which would enhance the mark for AO1. There is a clear effort to answer the question at the end **c** but again to boost AO2 the candidate ought to have explained and developed the point more fully and made explicit reference to increased political participation that ballot initiatives offer. There is also some imprecision at the start **d** when ballot initiatives are just described as 'common' rather than noting that the situation varies from state to state reflecting the federal nature of the USA. The candidate should have been more aware too of how powerful pressure groups are often behind ballot initiatives. There is also some confusion **e** when the candidate assumes senators and congressmen may not care about these issues — it would be worth noting that legislators do often support ballot initiatives, and that they provide an additional forum for democratic engagement by voters. The answer would also benefit from being less descriptive in places, which would boost AO2, and being clearer and better structured to gain marks for AO3.

(b) 'An outdated eighteenth-century device still used for the election of the twenty-first-century president.' Critically assess the role of the Electoral College. (30 marks)

(e) The question calls for a critical assessment, so your answer should work through several problems that are known to be associated with the role of the Electoral College in presidential selection, using evidence and examples wherever possible from past elections. However, the question also allows you to defend the role of the Electoral College, therefore using arguments from both sides of the debate (AO2). Your answer should clearly demonstrate knowledge and understanding of the way the Electoral College actually works (AO1), in order to provide context, as well as explaining why, despite known problems, it is still used, including the difficulties involved in any reform.

A-grade answer

(b) The 2000 election clearly showed the Electoral College (EC) to be the main factor in the election of the president. Due to the closeness of Bush and Gore in Florida the president was essentially chosen by the voters in that state, and only 500 votes separated the two. When we also remember that Bush, the victor, actually gained fewer popular votes than Gore, we can see that the EC has the potential to distort the public will **b d** e.

The EC is undoubtedly an antiquated device. The Founding Fathers devised it to ensure that the general voting population didn't have too much power. Of course, since then the EC has become much more democratic **a**. All of the electors, with only a rare transgressor, vote for the candidate that their state has voted for **d**.

So the system has been changed to ensure that voters actually have an impact on the decision. Having removed the original purpose of the system — to limit the impact of voters — the USA is now left with a pointless device that distorts public opinion for choosing its chief executive.

The EC system converts the public vote in each state into EC votes. Most states give all their votes to one candidate (although Maine and Nebraska allocate them proportionately), which means that someone who gains 51% of the vote in a state carries 100% of the EC votes of that state, with nothing for the loser **b**.

Although it is clear that there are problems with this system, we must also remember that there are reasons why it remains in place **c**. The central reason goes back to the creation of the system in eighteenth-century Philadelphia. The major conflict when the American constitution was being drawn up was the extent to which the federal government had power over the individual states **a**. Because of the fear that states would lose their power, a number of concessions were made to the smaller states **c**. First, each state was given equal representation in the Senate, regardless of size or population. To ensure that small states did not then wield disproportionate influence, the House of Representatives was apportioned seats on the basis of population **b**. As the number of EC votes per state is dependent on the number of congressmen in each state, even the smallest state is assured 3 votes in the EC, with the largest state, California, having 55. The magic number needed to win is 270 out of 538, and this can be achieved by winning as many states as possible, especially the ones with large EC votes **b**. This means that candidates concentrate their campaigning strategies on these crucial states and try to appeal to the voters within them **c**.

The EC system ensures that the smaller states are not totally ignored, yet even this idea can be seen as outdated, as it limits the voting power of those who live in the states with larger populations **c**. A voter in Wyoming actually has more power over who wins their state than a voter in California. However, candidates are obviously going to concentrate more of their efforts on winning bigger states, particularly the swing states **e** such as Ohio as their large number of EC votes — and the fact that they can go either way — gives them a much greater chance of winning the presidency **c**.

Although there are both advantages and disadvantages to a system that allows smaller states to have at least some impact on the outcome, it is hard to argue that people were happy that 2000 saw the most popular candidate in the country defeated and a president elected without a clear popular mandate **d**.

However, we must remember that this is a rarity. The last time it occurred before 2000 was in 1888 **a b**. Since then, the only distortion of the result by the EC had seemed to be in giving the winner a greater margin of victory, so there is little urgency in calls to change the system **c**. In 2012 for example, Obama won both the EC by 332–206 and the popular vote (51–47%). It can be said in defence of the EC that in the fragmented political landscape of the USA **e** it provides a basis of stability by helping to eliminate third-party candidates who cannot win concentrated support **c** and by giving one candidate a clear-cut majority and the legitimacy and mandate to rule **c**. However, it is hard to imagine how people would feel if the next election saw the leader of the free world chosen by the elected representatives in the House despite the fact that a majority of voters in the country as a whole had clearly chosen one candidate over the other.

Finally, it can be argued that perhaps there is a place for the EC in twenty-first-century US politics, although it may need reforming in the future if problems such as those of 2000 recur.

---

e **a** This student is able to place the Electoral College in a historical context to explain its workings, demonstrating contextual and historical awareness, and **b** there is clear understanding of the way that it works to elect the president, so AO1 marks would be high. **c** There is a good attempt to provide a critical evaluation through analysis of the workings of the EC, although **d** there are some undeveloped explanations, such as why some rogue electors do not vote the way their state does and why this is criticised, and how and why the EC system distorts the popular will. Generally, though, the response is focused and analytical and attempts to present both sides of the argument, with supporting evidence such as the figures from the 2012 election, thus achieving good AO2 marks. **e** The use of impressive and relevant political vocabulary, such as popular mandate, campaigning strategies, swing states and fragmented political landscape also raises the AO3 communication mark. Some parts of the answer lack development and clear explanation, but overall the response would certainly be worthy of an A grade.

C-grade answer

(b) The Electoral College (EC) has been widely criticised as a way of electing the president of the USA. It can cause a distortion of results through allowing a candidate with fewer overall votes to win, giving smaller parties little representation, and putting the election in the hands of electors who cast their respective votes.

Each state is assigned a certain amount of EC votes, depending on its population. By itself this is the fairest method of doing things. The number of votes for each presidential candidate is totalled, and the candidate with the most votes is assigned all of the EC votes for that particular state **a**. This means that a candidate can receive, for example, ten fewer votes out of 1 million than the other candidate and receive no seats whatsoever for that achievement **b**. The candidate with the highest number of EC votes wins the election as happened in 2012. A few

weeks after the election, with the results in, electors for each state, who are party members or officials, will meet in the capital of the state. Each will cast their EC vote depending on who won the state. However, electors are not required by law to vote for who actually won the state a. They can vote for whoever they please, so the trust of a large number of voters in a state is put in one person who may turn out to be a 'faithless elector' and vote for an entirely different candidate c.

The first major criticism of the EC system is that an overall winner, with the largest amount of votes in the country, can lose the election to someone who has won more votes in the EC. This happened in the 2000 election between Bush and Gore. Gore received more votes overall, but Bush performed better in terms of the EC and so won the presidential election. Due to complications in Florida over votes, the decision was taken to the Supreme Court, which ruled in favour of Bush c.

This brings me to the problem of getting rid of the EC. The fact is that because the EC was written into the constitution in the eighteenth century, it requires an amendment to change it, which is extremely difficult. An amendment to the constitution also requires that two-thirds of Congress and three-quarters of the states agree to it before it can be implemented. Therefore, it seems as though there is no alternative to the EC at the moment c.

Another drawback of the EC is that smaller parties get little or no representation b. Their support is scattered across the country, and unlike the Democrats and Republicans, who have strongholds in particular areas, they do not have enough concentrated support in one area to win a state and receive the EC votes. For example, in 2000 Ralph Nader received 19% of the overall votes but received a tiny proportion of representation because of it d.

Is the EC outdated now, or has it simply always been as distorting and unfair as this? What alternatives are there?

It could be argued that the world as a whole, and therefore the USA too, is more liberal than it was in the eighteenth century. Therefore, electors in the eighteenth century may not have exercised the 'freedom of speech' now exercised by the 'faithless electors', however rare they are c.

Three hundred years do not change the fact that the EC will distort results — the same system is still used. Therefore, it may not be a fair argument to say that the twenty-first century requires a better system than the eighteenth century did — the same problems are still there.

The EC does act like a first-past-the-post system, but only within each state and in a more distorting way than a simple first-past-the-post system. The beauty of a first-past-the-post system is that it is simple for voters to understand: they just cast their vote and hope their candidate wins the state. A straightforward first-past-the-post system like the UK's would not help the situation of the USA too much and would not be worth the effort of implementing it b. However, any other system of electing may be harder for voters to understand and may lower turnout further. Therefore, it seems that the USA is stuck with the EC.

In conclusion, I would not necessarily agree that the system is outdated. It has generally presented the same problems today as it would have done 300 years ago — distortion of results, faithless electors and little representation of smaller parties.

However, it is hard to suggest an alternative, as the constitution implements the EC and is very difficult to change. Even if there were an alternative it might not be any better than the current system and would present problems of its own e.

(e) This student produces a very mixed response to the question: a there is accuracy on some of the workings of the Electoral College and a clear attempt to engage with the question, but at the same time there is little coherent structure or developed analysis, however good some of the specific arguments are. b At times there is little clarity of argument, such as the mention of presidential candidates winning 'seats' or the arguments relating to first-past-the-post or why the system produces distortions. Also, it is not a problem that minor parties are 'unrepresented', as there is only one president. c Other arguments are not fully developed: for example, why are 'faithless electors' criticised, what caused the result in 2000, and why would a constitutional amendment be hard to achieve? d There are some factual errors (e.g. Nader's 19% of the vote in 2000), all of which suggest a less than firm grasp of the EC system. e The conclusion is very vague. Nevertheless, the student manages to get across just enough AO1 knowledge and AO2 critical assessment to reach a low C grade, although the communication mark (AO3) would not be high.

Question 2 Political parties

(a) Why are US parties often described as 'organisationally weak'? (10 marks)

ⓔ The answer to this question should focus on the relative weakness of US parties as de-centralised organisations (possibly compared with the stronger, centralised UK parties), with some evidence of this weakness, such as their lack of control over candidate selection or over their elected candidates. No reference to party ideology or party renewal is required. An explanation of why parties are weak organisations in the USA, such as the constitutional separation of powers or federalism, would be essential for the higher mark bands.

A-grade answer

(a) The doctrine of the separation of powers and the system of federalism used in the USA encourage political parties that may be considered 'organisationally weak' **b**. In the USA there is a significant fragmentation of power **d** (introduced by the Founding Fathers in order to ensure no area of government dominated the political process), and consequently parties are forced to span a wide range of political institutions **b**. At a state level, parties need representatives, e.g. as governors or in state legislatures, yet equally parties have to make their mark in Washington at the federal level **a**. Parties in the USA must make their voices heard in the federal legislature and gain a hold over the executive, i.e. the presidency. This is not helped by the fact that like the UK, the USA has a bicameral legislature, i.e. the House of Representatives and the Senate. In order to exert most influence, political parties must gain power at all levels of government. As a result the party machine must be incredibly vast, which leads to organisational weaknesses **b**.

The need for a large party machine is enhanced by America's geography. The USA is a huge area, which means parties have to work hard to cover the whole country. In covering all areas geographically and politically, the party inevitably becomes fragmented **b**. Moreover, it is noteworthy that major parties meet in their entirety only once every 4 years, at the national party convention during a presidential election. This event has been declining in significance in recent years and consequently there is little opportunity for party unity to be significantly strengthened; the focus, after all, is on the selection of a president, not the day-to-day running of the party **a**.

Finally, weak party discipline in the USA would encourage the idea of ineffective party organisation **a**. Voting across party lines in Congress is common (although reduced in recent years), demonstrating that US parties are relatively uncoordinated. This is unlike the UK, where strict party discipline is enforced via the party whips **c**.

Although there are reasons for organisationally weak parties in the USA, there is also an argument that this is necessary. US parties are essentially 'broad coalitions': they contain, for example, moderates like Romney (Republican) and Obama (Democrat), while also having a more conservative wing. Essentially, therefore, stronger party organisation would give parties a narrower appeal and as a consequence potentially alienate large 'voting blocs' or proportions of the electorate **b d**.

It has therefore been argued that symptoms of weak organisation, e.g. issue-centred or candidate-centred election campaigns a d are deliberate, as parties attempt to gain a maximum number of votes.

Historically, the American parties have always encompassed a range of diverse groups spanning the entire country, e.g. the New Deal policies of Roosevelt in the 1930s, uniting white southerners, African-Americans and blue-collar manual workers. Consequently, it can be argued parties may appear organisationally weak yet it would be impossible to perceive any other alternative, considering the nature of the constitution (separation of powers) and the previous success of parties acting as 'broad coalitions' or 'big umbrellas' d.

(e) This student's answer is a strongly analytical response covering a lot of ground. b It clearly shows why parties are weaker in the USA, thus gaining AO2 marks, and a demonstrates AO1 knowledge of some (but not all) of their organisational characteristics. The student backs up the arguments with convincing evidence and wide-ranging examples, and c also makes a synoptic passing reference to the UK for comparison. d The answer is communicated coherently and with structure, including excellent political vocabulary such as fragmentation of power, issue and candidate-centred campaigns and broad coalitions, although it could have been more succinct in parts. It would achieve a high grade A.

C-grade answer

(a) The best expression of national organisation by the two US parties comes in the national conventions, the most public manifestation of the parties. Although the conventions show organisation, they only occur every 4 years, lasting for 4 days, and there is not much opportunity for all the 4,000 delegates who attend to have their say a. Despite being organised to pick the presidential candidate and the running mate and to decide the party platform, the convention has become less formal and less important. The decline in organisation may be a result of their diminishing importance: it is suggested they merely confirm the presidential candidate and running mate. Their poor organisation can be seen in the fact that in 1963 the terrestrial channels put in 46 hours of coverage of the Republican convention, while in 2000 the same channels managed just 10.5 hours!

The national conventions are also used to decide the party platform, but the weak organisation of this was shown in 1992. One of the planks of the Republican Party platform was 'We believe the unborn child has a fundamental right to life', but they then went on to call for a human life amendment to the constitution. A CBS poll found that only 7% of voters approved of this plank, thus the convention was organised well enough to be able to make unpopular decisions to go on the party platform a.

Parties' main functions are fund-raising, organisation, communication and policy formation a, but their failure to fulfil these functions means they have to some extent been usurped by pressure groups, political action committees and the media. The weak organisation of the parties has to some extent been forgotten about, in that politicians communicate to the voters through the media and the voters speak back to them through opinion polls, so the role of the parties is cut out a.

ⓔ a Despite initially focusing the answer almost exclusively on the roles of the national conventions, meaning a very limited response, the student does demonstrate some AO1 knowledge of party organisation through this description. However, the answer does not really get to grips with the wider question, showing little AO2 analysis of why parties are organisationally weaker in the USA and not giving evidence to show that they are by indicating other organisational characteristics. Although the last paragraph makes enough valid and creditable points, and demonstrates sufficient knowledge of party conventions to just reach a low grade C, overall the answer lacks the clear and convincing understanding of the main reasons for party weakness which could have gained higher AO2 marks and led to a higher grade. The answer could also have been more clearly communicated to achieve higher AO3 communication marks.

(b) Consider the reasons for the strength of the two-party system and the insignificance of third parties in the USA.

(30 marks)

ⓔ In your response you should give reasons why, in a country as large and diverse as the USA, there are only two parties effectively competing at all levels of government. Answers should span a number of different explanations, from the strength of partisan identification through to funding advantages, the 'big tent' nature of the parties and the effects of the electoral system. Examples and evidence are expected in support of both two-party strength and third-party insignificance in elections. However, students at the higher levels of response may challenge either the insignificance of third parties, by pointing to their successes or impact, or the strength of the two-party system, by noting that (unlike the position in the UK) the two main parties are very different in each of the 50 states.

A-grade answer

(b) Although it is certainly true that a key characteristic of the US political system has been the insignificance of third-party candidates, it is possible to argue that in some cases they do succeed in their aims, and that the two-party political system is not as strong as it might seem **b**.

First, let us consider the evidence in favour of the strength of the two-party system. It should be noted that not since 1856 has a president not been a member of either the Democratic or Republican party **a**. Furthermore, these two parties currently dominate the federal legislature. Out of 100 senators, only two are independent (King and Sanders) and both caucus with the Democratic Party, and only one of 435 members of the House is independent of the two main parties **a**. This clearly indicates that the two major parties have maintained their strength, but the question this raises is: why?

Perhaps the most obvious reason is the first-past-the-post electoral system used in all US elections. According to this system, all seats (and Electoral College votes) are awarded to the candidate who gets the most votes. This means that third parties are at a tremendous disadvantage, for even if they gain a substantial portion of the vote they are unlikely to achieve any seats in the legislature or votes for the presidency **b**. For example, although Ross Perot gained 19% of the vote in the presidential election of 1992, he was not able to win any Electoral College votes at all **a**. The only small parties that do gain from this system are the regionally based parties, as they can rely on concentrated support a b. Thus in 1968, George Wallace and the American Independence Party gained 13% of the vote and 45 Electoral College votes, as they were able to hold much of the South a. Because of the regional nature of these parties, they cannot hope to gain enough broad support to challenge either the Republicans or the Democrats, and so the first-past-the-post system has been of tremendous benefit to the strength of the two-party system b c.

Another significant factor in this success has been the flexibility of the two main parties working over huge geographical areas, with one of the most diverse populations on earth a. The USA's Democratic and Republican parties cover a whole range of interests and political philosophies. Both parties have liberal and conservative wings, and so can appeal to broad sections of the public b c. Third parties such as the Socialists or the Libertarian Party tend to be on the fringes of the US political scene and find it difficult to convince enough of the electorate to support them a.

Furthermore, the political system itself favours the Democrats and Republicans and the preservation of the two-party system in a number of ways.

First, states have many different rules regarding who gets to appear on the ballot. While it is possible to appear on the ballot in Alabama with 25 signatures, other states require a much higher figure or even a percentage (e.g. 5%) of the state's population a. For an unknown party this can be very difficult, as it means collecting millions of signatures and spending huge amounts of money, usually with little to show for it b.

This leads to the issue of campaign finance. It is not possible to gain matched funding c from the federal government unless you have gained 5% of the popular vote at the last election a. This means that while the two big parties always gain funding, a party would have to have been successful in a previous election before it could gain enough votes or money to be successful b. In other words, the system is heavily disadvantageous for third parties and clearly favours the two main parties. Only Ross Perot and the Reform Party have been able to claim funding, and then only in 1996 and 2000 a.

Beyond this there are other factors at work, and it is very difficult for a third party to gain enough money from private donors to establish itself. As the system and structure of American politics and society is so disadvantageous b few are likely to give resources or financial assistance: it would mean backing an almost certain loser. But until they gain such financial assistance, third parties are likely to continue to lose b.

The media too have not been helpful to third parties and have tended to reinforce the strength of the two-party system. The media, particularly the television networks and cable channels such as NBC and CNN, are unlikely to mention candidates from smaller parties, as they cannot see them as successful a. Such candidates consequently find it much more difficult to get their message across than the Republicans and the Democrats b. Furthermore, only once has a presidential candidate from outside the two main parties been able to take part in a presidential debate, and since then the American people have only been presented with a simple choice between two candidates a. Additionally, the cost of television advertising

(unlike the UK, the US system offers no free broadcasting time for parties) makes it difficult for parties already starved of funds to gain public attention **b**.

One reason why all these disadvantages have remained in place is the difficulty in bringing about change in the USA. In order to remove many of these obstacles to third parties, for example introducing a presidential election system without the distorting EC, would require either a constitutional amendment or successful votes in the states, both notoriously difficult to achieve **a b**. Even after talks about change following the Gore–Bush controversy in 2000, little has been done to make serious reforms, as the current system benefits the two main parties so much **b**.

Finally, many in America consider the two-party system desirable as it ensures (usually) a winner who gets more than 50% of the vote. Since 1916 the Republicans and the Democrats have never had less than 80% of the vote between them, which is in stark contrast to the 60–65% attained by Labour and the Conservatives in the UK **d**. In such a large and diverse country, many consider it preferable to have an obvious winner with a majority, as it promotes consensus **c** and this can only be attained in a two-party system.

In conclusion, although some argue America is not a two-party system, but is instead perhaps a 100-party system, it is undeniable that the strength and durability of the Republican and Democratic dominance of US politics has survived because of the system, media, money and ideology **e**.

ⓔ b This is a well-focused and wide-ranging response to the question, and the focus, which starts in the introduction, is maintained throughout the essay, which has a coherent structure (AO3) and contains a lot of convincing AO2 analysis and evaluation. **a** The AO1 knowledge and understanding is impressive and **d** the response includes synoptic reference to the UK for comparison, with almost every argument backed up by relevant evidence and examples of both the two main parties and a number of different third parties and their impact. The answer is very well communicated, **c** using political concepts and vocabulary, and **e** culminates in a conclusion, so the AO3 mark would be high. This answer would gain a high grade A.

C-grade answer

(b) The USA has always had a two-party system. From the historic days of Washington and Jefferson establishing the two parties, third parties or Independents have never had any influence, and although recent years have seen attempts to achieve this, e.g. by Ross Perot (19%), the restriction of the electoral system and broad coalitions have stopped this. In the light of this, can the US system be deemed a two-party system, or are third parties slowly gaining more popularity?

In the two parties of Democrats and Republicans numerous factions appear. As Bennett said, you don't just get 'Democrats' or 'Republicans' as party labels. Many are termed 'liberal Democrats' or 'conservative Republicans', and in 2000 Bush called himself a 'compassionate conservative' **a**. This demonstrates the 'broad church' system of the two parties, which enables them to exclude third parties that cannot fit their policies into an ideological gap in the US electorate **b**. From the Rockefeller Republicans to the conservative Republicans to the southern

Democrats (Clinton and Gore) to the old left (Dukakis), all the parties have internal conflicting factions representing different ideologies a. Rockefellers such as Ford were more Democrat-inclined, promoting bigger government etc. However, you also had the conservatives like Reagan etc. who were more traditional Republicans, believing in tax cuts etc. A recent development of the Democrats with Clinton's New Deal d demonstrated the centralisation of the two main parties, with Clinton trying to get rid of 'big government' under the influence of growing public opinion, giving substance to Mark Shields' point that 'they are two parties separated by the issue of abortion'.

It is this ideological engulfment of the whole US electoral spectrum that prevents third-party success but also ensures their durability b. When Anderson was campaigning in 1980, President Nixon announced the 'southern strategy' to attract all his voters d. The same thing happened with Ross Perot, which made Clinton and others do lots of reforms, so that his popularity suffered heavily.

However, is this insignificance of third parties really true? In recent years, since the time of Anderson, third-party candidates have in turn affected and influenced the vote. In 1992 Perot took a lot of Republican voters, resulting in a Democrat victory, while Nader in 2004, while only gaining 1%, still managed to take vital votes in a tight race of 271–266 a d!

It can be said that third parties never intend to be that significant and most are just temporary, created to provide an outlet for disillusioned voters (with the exception of Ross Perot in 1992 and 1996) b.

However, is this attitude of just influencing and being more like electoral pressure groups b than political parties forced by the restrictions of the US system? It can be said that the Electoral College system actually is not in proportion to the amount of votes won. Ross Perot gained 19% of the vote but because they were evenly spread over states he gained no Electoral College votes a. One governor did manage to gain 13 EC votes, mainly because his vote was concentrated in the southern states, which still didn't make a significant impact. Reforms such as the Maine system and automatic plan didn't even give much hope for any renewed third-party significance.

However, can we ever deem the American system a two-party system, with Broder actually stating 'the party's over'? This expands on the fact that the USA can be seen as a 50-party system. Federalism and state powers and the fact that they only meet nationally every 4 years means that they can be split up into geographical factions, as the Republicans' policy in Arkansas will be different to that in Connecticut a b. One case study showed that they declared in Arkansas 'protection for all God-fearing families', but Connecticut watered down these policies and promised 'good education'!

But is this such a big problem in America? The liberal democracy and the Constitution ensure that congressmen are elected on issue lines more than on party lines, unlike MPs in the UK. This brings in Edmund Burke's theory of representative or delegate. As one political scientist said, congressmen 'take party lines first, but they become second when the election is over' and constituent pressure is much more of an issue c.

> Though there are some claims of party renewal, many claim that the Democrats 'six for 06' campaign helped to develop the parties c.
>
> The American Congress shows the US system is not that of party government, and carrots and sticks cannot be used to such a high degree as in the UK, so despite their presence the American system can be said to force this culture of 'broad church' parties and that of insignificant third parties. What can be said of both political cultures is that, despite their differences, the significance of third parties is rising, with the UK's Liberal Democrats gaining their highest number of seats in 2005 (66) and Ross Perot and Nader in the USA causing some interesting results e. This may indicate the changing scene of both party systems and their prospective durability.

ⓔ Although this answer would not gain high AO3 marks for communication, as it is not well structured or fully coherent, it does attempt to communicate some interesting and relevant AO2 arguments. However, most of these remain undeveloped. The student has a lot of knowledge but c it is not always directly linked to the question and frequently drifts (e.g. into Burke's theory or Electoral College reform) and arguments only tenuously related to the question are introduced, such as party decline and renewal. d It also contains several errors, such as 'Clinton's New Deal', Nixon's southern strategy in 1980, and Nader's 2004 result. It also lacks examples from recent elections such as 2008 and 2012. However, there is relevant analysis in the answer, such as b the broad church nature of the parties and the electoral system effect, backed up with relevant examples (Perot and Nader) and a using specific evidence from voting statistics, as well as e an attempt to bring in some comparative material from the UK. This just pushes this answer into the C grade. Higher marks could have been achieved if the student had focused more on the actual question and excluded scattergun arguments lacking relevance to the question, which apart from wasting precious time indicate a lack of understanding of what the question is asking the student to do. Some parts of the answer would have been more relevant to (a) than (b), but they cannot be allocated marks if they are in the wrong section.

Question 3 **Voting behaviour**

(a) How important is party identification (partisanship) in explaining US voting behaviour?   (10 marks)

ⓔ This question calls for a clear definition and explanation of the term itself and a focus on why and whether it is important in explaining why Americans vote the way they do. It demands some knowledge of the long-term (primacy) factors affecting voting behaviour and the agencies of political socialisation, and also some evidence of the decline of partisanship in recent years, with some explanation offered for this decline and its possible consequences in order to address the 'how important' part of the question.

A-grade answer

(a) The majority of American voters still have some form of long-term party identification, which is described as a deep-rooted attachment to one political party **a**. It is usually connected to a voter's political socialisation within the family leading them to become a Democrat or a Republican and subsequently to vote for that party throughout their life **a**. Party identification can be very strong, with the voter having a party loyalty throughout their life, or it can weaken as a result of other influences on their political thinking and behaviour, for example from their education or their occupation or from the influence of specific candidates or issues at elections, which may result in them changing their vote **a b**.

For example, it was said that many Democrats switched their vote to Reagan in 1980 and 1984 because they liked his personality and right-wing policies more than they did the Democrat ones. They were known as 'Reagan Democrats' **a c**. This weakening of party identification is called de-alignment **c**. Voters without a party identification are called Independents **c** — their vote can go either way, and both parties try to attract support from these voters while at the same time trying to keep the votes of their 'core' aligned supporters **a c**. It is thought that the number of independent voters fluctuates from election to election.

An example of voters with a strong party identification would have been southern Democrat voters until the 1960s, when they lost their strong identification with the Democratic Party because of its commitment to Civil Rights **a b**. Since that time, many white southern voters have identified with and switched to voting for the Republican Party. Because many voters now lack a strong identification with a party, they are less likely to turn out to vote, which has led to higher abstention in recent years — turnout in 2012 was under 60% of the eligible voters **b**. This is particularly true of 'weak' identifiers rather than 'strong' ones. Because US political parties are aware that partisanship is weakening in the electorate, they cannot rely on a solid base of voters turning out to vote for them. Their candidates now have to work harder to keep the support not only of their own voters but also of the de-aligned independent voters at each election **b c**.

This is an exceptionally well-argued response, demonstrating **a** a very clear understanding of the term, and is well communicated, with **c** use of political terms and concepts. It does not drift from the question, **b** addresses AO2 'importance' and remains focused throughout. Although no

statistical evidence is presented, this does not detract from the answer overall, which contains strong evidence and examples of partisanship as well as its decline. It would receive a high mark for all three assessment objectives and a top A grade.

C-grade answer

(a) Party identification is when voters link to parties and always vote for those parties no matter who the candidates are or what the issues are at that election **a**. Voters get their party identification from different things like their class or where they live in the USA, in the red states or the blue states **a**. Voters who are poor and have little education are likely to identify with the Democratic Party, as this is the one most likely to help them. Voters who come from richer classes and who have gone to university are more likely to be Republicans as they support lower taxes **a**.

American voters do not always keep a strong identification with a party, their circumstances may change and they may change their vote as a result. Women are more likely to be Democrat voters, but sometimes they switch to the Republicans because they do not agree with abortion or they are concerned about national security, like the 'security moms' who voted for Bush in 2004 **a**. However, most voters do identify with one party rather than another and will usually vote for that party, and if they are very strongly identified with a particular party they are never likely to change their voting behaviour. If parties do not manage to get their identified voters to turn out to vote it is possible that they will lose the election. That is why they concentrate on pleasing their voters rather than trying to win votes from the 'other side' in their campaigns **b**.

ⓔ **a** While this answer does not fully explain the sources of partisan alignment and identification, it does try to explain the term and gives examples of aligned voters. **b** It is also quite focused, but it lacks the extra analysis and evidence, political vocabulary and communication that would take it into higher assessment objective levels. It would, however, gain a C grade largely as a result of the AO1 marks.

(b) How far is voting behaviour in the US determined by gender, age and religion?   (30 marks)

ⓔ This question requires a focus on all three characteristics mentioned, roughly in equal proportions (though it need not be exact). Top grade answers will have plenty of recent statistics to back up the points made, and also (briefly) allude to other factors not stated in the title so as to provide a broader perspective, whilst not going off at a tangent and discussing all aspects of voting behaviour in great detail.

A-grade answer

(b) Voting behaviour in the US, as indeed in most democracies, is determined by a wide range of factors, and age, gender and religion are clearly important aspects of a voter's profile. While they clearly give many indications of how a person might vote, they also need to be seen alongside other factors such as race, income and indeed the conduct of the campaign itself and the personalities of the candidates.

When considering age, the general principle is that older voters are more likely to vote Republican. In 2012 for example, Romney won 56% of the 65+ vote, but only 37%

AQA A2 Government & Politics

of those aged under 30 a. By contrast, it has been fairly common in recent elections for young voters to 'trend Democrat'. There are several possible explanations, above all perhaps because the Democrats are the more progressive/liberal party on social issues such as abortion and gay rights. Republicans by contrast are more conservative on such matters, which may turn off younger voters. Obama in 2008 paid special attention to attracting the youth vote and made extensive and very effective use of the new social media such as Facebook and created his own social networking site, mybarackobama.com. It should also be noted that racial minorities (especially Hispanics) are more numerous among younger voters, and racial minorities are also much more likely to vote Democrat. Age, however, needs to be seen alongside other factors such as wealth, race and religion as a guide to how Americans vote.

When it comes to religion, the general picture is that the more religious voters are, the more likely they are to vote Republican and vice versa. In 2012, Romney won by 59% to 39% among those who said they go to church regularly, while Obama won by 62% to 34% a among those who never go to a religious service. This in part reflects age (religious people are more likely to be older), but also the platforms of each party. Many Republicans associate themselves with the 'religious right' who oppose gay marriage, welcome prayers in school and sometimes even want creationism taught. White evangelical Protestants in particular are likely to vote Republican — 78% in 2012 a. Interestingly though, the bulk of the Jewish vote goes to the Democrats d, so it is too simplistic to say religious people always favour the GOP. In addition, many churchgoers especially from black Pentecostal churches and more liberal Christian denominations will vote Democrat either because of race or because their own beliefs are more progressive. More non-religious people tend to vote Democrat because of their weaker formal links with religious groups especially evangelicals. Democrats tend to be more pro-choice and in favour of retaining a clear separation between the state and religion as laid down in the constitution, which appeals to non-religious people and more liberal Christians.

Gender also produces a very clear and interesting divide — the so-called 'gender gap' whereby more women consistently vote Democrat, while the opposite is true for men. In 2012, Obama won the female vote by a margin of 55% to 44% while Romney won the male vote with a polling advantage of 52% to 45%. Many political scientists believe this is due to the different appeals of the two parties. The Democrats are generally viewed as more compassionate and pro-women (EMILY's List and pro-choice) while the Republicans are seen as less interested in women's rights and more in favour of an aggressive foreign policy and higher military spending (especially under Bush 2000–08) which appeals more to men. Also, some Republican candidates for Congress in 2012, such as Todd Akin e, put off women voters by comments such as 'legitimate rape'. Their stronger support for gun control also attracts more men than women. There are, however, always exceptions to the rule (Sarah Palin and 'hockey moms' in 2008) so one must not make sweeping statements here. Gender too needs to be seen alongside other aspects of a voter's profile.

Overall though, while age, religion and gender are undoubtedly very important in explaining voter behaviour, one also has to consider other factors as well. Race is especially important in the US c, with African-Americans voting overwhelmingly for the Democrats (90%+) b, while whites strongly favour the Republicans. This is in

part due to history (the black vote has been solidly Democrat since the 1930s and the New Deal Coalition) and also to the platforms of the two parties. The Democrats for instance were widely associated with bringing in civil rights laws in the 1960s. There are also the candidates' personalities and the conduct of the campaign to consider **c**. In 2012 for example, Romney lost some support due to his campaign gaffes such as implying the Republicans did not care about 47% of voters, while in 2004, Kerry was successfully portrayed as weak and ineffectual. One should not forget the importance of issues as well, especially the state of the economy. As Clinton noted in 1992, 'It's the economy stupid.' **c**. Voters do not just vote because of who they are but also because of how they feel about key issues and which candidate they trust the most.

In summary, gender, age and religion do have a major influence on how Americans vote. If you are young, female and an atheist you are likely to vote Democrat; if you are an African-American too it will almost be definite. By contrast, an elderly white male churchgoer is most probably a Republican. They are, however, only part of the reasons that explain voting behaviour in the US. Arguably, race and the personality of the candidates are just as important. The issues, personalities of the candidates and conduct of the campaign also cannot be ignored. Voting behaviour is a complex issue, so therefore one must not exaggerate the impact of one factor above another.

ⓔ This is a very well focused and knowledgeable answer. Particularly good are the frequent and accurate quoting of figures from the 2012 election **a**, and even where **b** the candidate offers a more general figure, that is easily forgiven, such is the grasp of figures elsewhere. There are also several places **c**, where the answer shows detailed knowledge of other factors that help explain voting behaviour, but the answer does not go into unnecessary length and detail about these. The unexpected but entirely valid reference to the Jewish vote **d** also gains credit. Most answers would only comment on more obvious examples such as the evangelical vote, and this reference makes a nice contrast to the general rule, showing the deeper complexities of the issue. The precise reference to congressional elections **e** also adds a breadth to the answer, which is about voting behaviour in general, not just for presidential elections. All this knowledge is relevantly used for developed explanation, which would gain high marks for AO1 and AO2. The conclusion also brings the various strands together well and sees the three factors stated in the title as only part of a more complex picture. The answer is also consistently focused on the title and is clearly structured enabling it to score highly on AO2 and AO3.

C-grade answer

(b) Gender, age and religion are all important to how people vote in America. If you are religious you are much more likely to vote Republican, especially if you are 'born again'. This is because the Republicans are much more in favour of policies that many Christians support. This includes being anti-abortion and gay marriages, and wanting more religion in public life **a**. Fewer religious people (who are on the increase in America) are much more likely to vote Democrat **b**. Democrats favour a church/state separation and see religion as a private matter.

It is similar with age. The older you are, the more likely you are to vote for Romney and the Republicans, especially if you are over 65 **b**. Young people by contrast strongly backed Obama in 2008 and 2012, partly because he seemed youthful himself, but also because he made good use of social media such as Facebook to get supporters. Young people are however much less likely to vote because of political alienation and apathy. A lot of effort has been put in to improve turnout among them such as 'Rock the Vote' but they are still the age group least likely to vote and most apathetic about politics **c**.

The Democrats also have more policies that appeal to young people such as healthcare reforms (Obamacare) **f** and being pro-gay.

Women are much more likely to vote Democrat/Obama as well. This is because they support women's rights such as abortion, and include high profile women such as Hillary Clinton and Nancy Pelosi. Hillary Clinton almost became Democrat candidate in 2008. By contrast, the Republicans are often seen as sexist and full of 'old white men' though Sarah Palin was an exception (obviously!) **h** in 2008. They often oppose abortion and some of their members even seem to believe that raping women is not always wrong.

However, there are lots of other reasons why people in the US vote how they do apart from age, religion and gender. Race is a very important factor too. Around 95% **d** of blacks voted for Obama in 2008 and 2012, while a majority of whites favoured Romney. Hispanics also favour the Democrats, and as they are growing rapidly this is bad news for the Republicans. Minorities favour the Democrats because they are seen as the party most supportive of them (civil rights etc.) and a lot of it goes back to the New Deal Coalition. People are also influenced by things like television ads and the policies of the candidates **e**. As candidates spend huge amounts of money during elections, this too affects how people vote especially with 'attack ads', which are forms of negative campaigning. Attack ads are now much more common because of the rise of Super PACs.

So, it is not just about gender, age and religion but they are still important. Old men who go to church (and own a gun!) **g h** are far more likely to vote for the Republicans than a young, black women who rarely goes to church.

e This answer has the potential for a higher grade as it does focus on the question asked, straightaway referring to all three factors, and some development of all the reasons is attempted **a**. Yet there are several places where there is a real lack of detail or examples **b**. This restricts the number of marks that can be awarded for AO1. For example, an examiner would expect to know why precisely non-religious electors are more likely to vote Democrat, and older ones Republican. This also hinders the quality of analysis, which reduces the marks awarded for AO2. There is also a section **c** that is not really relevant when the candidate discusses youth and election turnouts. The main area that would enhance the quality of this answer though, would be the inclusion of plenty of recent voting figures to support the assertions made in the essay. This would boost the marks for AO1 considerably. The only figure quoted **d** is not actually anything to do with the three factors referred to in the question. The answer would gain some credit for explaining that there are other factors that help explain voting patterns **e**, but again these are not developed at any length and with only brief illustrative examples. There is also a misunderstanding **f** about young people being more favourable to Obamacare. Not only is this not supported by any evidence, it is actually a rather misleading generalisation to make, which limits the amount of marks that can be awarded for AO1. It is also unwise to add in new material such as gun ownership **g** right at the end of the answer. Stylistically, the answer as well as being brief, also suffers from the unnecessary use of exclamation marks **h**, which do not really add much to the overall tone of the answer.

Question 4 **Pressure groups**

(a) Explain the growth of pressure group activity in recent years. (10 marks)

🄔 The focus here must be on reasons for the increased activity of pressure groups in the USA and nothing else. Students may go back to the 1960s, when pressure group activity began to grow significantly, to offer valid explanations for this growth. Examples and evidence of new pressure group activity, such as the civil rights movement, the pro- and anti-abortion groups after *Roe* v *Wade* and new social movements arising from the emergence of political issues such as environmentalism and feminism, should be included in the explanation wherever possible. Any other consideration of pressure group activity is not required and would not be rewarded.

A-grade answer

(a) The growth in pressure group activity, particularly since the 1960s, is the result of many factors. It can certainly be seen as part of a growth of direct democracy with increasing use of initiatives, referendums and notably issue groups **b**. In a climate of falling turnout due to voter apathy and lack of political efficacy **c**, pressure groups seemed set to increase in activity and popularity as they offered an opportunity for genuine participation **b** and the ability to get new issues onto the agenda **b**. For example, Civil Rights legal changes in the 1960s were the work of the National Association for the Advancement of Colored People (NAACP) **a**. This effectiveness of pressure groups increased their popularity and more began to grow **b**. Pressure groups benefited from the numerous access points due to the decentralised federal system and the weak, fragmented party system **d**.

Pressure groups also grew and benefited from the USA's participatory political culture **b c**. Pressure groups benefited at a time when many people were less committed to conventional political activism and participation, as evidenced by partisan de-alignment **b c** (the number of people classifying themselves as Independents rose from 6% to 40% between 1952 and 2011) and by falling turnout and party membership **b**.

The general period of relative affluence and prosperity created by the welfare state allowed and encouraged an emphasis on new environmental and social problems **b**, e.g. the creation of the Sierra Club **a**. This growing concern over new problems replaced the economic worries which had dominated in previous times **b**. Also the growth of 'sleaze' and the decline in the attractiveness of politicians as a result of Nixon and the Watergate scandal in the 1970s led to the trend towards pressure group involvement and other such concerns **e**.

🄔 **b** Although by no means providing a perfectly focused answer, this student does specifically address the question and is able to offer several different and plausible explanations for the growth of pressure group activity. **a** There is also a good integration of evidence and examples such as the effectiveness of the NAACP and new problems such as environmentalism into the answer, which raises the AO1 and AO2 marks, along with **c** the use of political concepts and political vocabulary.

Good analytical points do not need to be over-argued: the argument that the effectiveness of pressure groups increased their popularity is concise and clear, although some other arguments would have benefited from greater clarity and further development, such as **d** the relationship of access points to growth. **e** The linkage of the Watergate scandal to the growth of pressure groups is an interesting one, as is the implied link between falling turnouts and pressure group activity, but both could have been developed further for higher AO2 marks. The range of explanations allows this response to reach a grade A.

C-grade answer

(a) The US federal system creates numerous access points for pressure groups where they can influence politicians, whether it be state legislatures, governors, Congress, the executive or the judiciary **c**. The USA has also always been a country of diverse interests: Floridians have different views to Alaskans, and Californian fruit-pickers have different opinions to Fortune 500 CEOs **c**. Interest groups are one of the only ways that everyone's views can be represented at the same level. Accompanying this is the fact that the two main parties are so broad and catch-all in their nature that they cannot represent the views of all their supporters at one time **b**. The work *The American Voter*, published in 1960, portrayed the US electorate as unsophisticated and generally uninterested in politics. This would change from the 1960s onwards as voters became more sophisticated and were able to clearly distinguish between the parties. This sophistication also led to an increase in the activity of pressure groups as more and more citizens participated through them **b**.

Pressure groups have also benefited from the proliferation of controversial and contentious issues **b** which separate rather than unite parties. Pressure groups campaign over questions such as abortion, gun control, gay rights, Civil Rights, women's rights and the environment. These issues have fuelled the increase in pressure group activity, including such examples as Emily's List, the Sierra Club, the League of Women Voters and many others **a b**.

The increase in PAC activity during the 1970s and 1980s was influenced by the Federal Election Act of 1974 and amendments made to it which eventually created the term 'soft money', whereby they could spend money unregulated by campaign finance laws **c**.

On the whole it is clear that pressure groups have exploded in number and that there has been a variety of causes of this.

e **b** It is clear from the answer that this student has a lot of knowledge of US pressure groups and at times is able to focus this on the question asked, so gaining some AO2 marks. **c** The main problem is the very over-generalised response that relates more to pressure group activity and fails to sustain a clear focus on growth. However, **b** the selection of one or two reasons, such as the growing sophistication of voters and new issues that attracted growing participation in pressure group activity, and **a** the many examples given, take the response into a C grade.

(b) Assess the factors that make some US pressure groups more successful than others in achieving their goals.

(30 marks)

ⓔ This question asks students to make evaluative judgements about the variables that influence pressure groups' success (or failure) and to assess the numerous factors involved in explaining why some pressure groups may successfully achieve their goals and others may not, perhaps at different times. It is therefore essential to focus on several factors to explain how and why successful pressure groups do achieve their goals, comparing them with those that are less successful. Examples of specific pressure groups and evidence of their 'successful' or 'unsuccessful' activities within the US political system are essential to achieve higher grades.

A-grade answer

(b) Some US pressure groups have been seen to achieve considerably more success than others. The reasons for such differences can be explained by a number of different factors **b**.

Commonly, the finances of pressure groups, or more specifically their financial wing, political action committees (PACs), and their ability to raise funds are of considerable importance **a**. As the costs of fighting elections increase for both presidential and congressional candidates, the importance of pressure group donations heightens **b**. Concerns over the amount of money contributed to political candidates by PACs were highlighted in the passing of the Federal Election Campaign Act 1974, which placed a number of restrictions on so-called 'hard money' **c**. Notably, any one PAC was prevented from donating more than $5,000 per annum under this legislation. Arguably, though, pressure groups are still able to exert massive influence through 'soft money', used to encourage potential voters for their favoured party to register, for example **a**. The arrival of Super PACs following the Citizens United decision in 2010 has opened the floodgates to even more money from interest groups.

A lot of commentary has highlighted the massive role pressure groups have played in party finance in the past. It has been questioned whether a system of 'cash for access' exists, where greater finances give groups greater political clout **b**. It is true that groups that tend to be more affluent, e.g. large oil companies, do appear to achieve more success. During his presidency George W. Bush was dogged by claims that he was linked too closely with energy corporations and the oil industry. The collapse of Enron is particularly noteworthy, as it highlighted the work Bush had done in commending Enron to the Indian government **d**.

That said, this argument has its critics. In the past, *Fortune* magazine, which conducts an annual survey of the most influential pressure groups, has frequently found that it is membership numbers rather than finance that give some groups the greater advantage **b**. Significantly, the American Association of Retired Persons has 33 million members and is often ranked highest in *Fortune's* survey. This argument is further supported by the relative success of the National Rifle Association, which has a 3 million membership of extremely pro-gun Americans **e**. This group played a key role arguably in stopping the passing of some gun control measures following the shootings at Sandy Hook in 2012.

The government in power is a further factor affecting the success of pressure groups. The Republicans, for example, tend to be pro-gun and anti-abortion. A Republican-dominated Congress, therefore, is more likely to listen to the professional lobbying of the NRA or National Right to Life Committee when passing legislation. Notably, pressure group influence on the federal executive is subject to change, depending on the ideological persuasion of the incumbent president a b.

Furthermore, if a group can become part of an 'iron triangle' it is likely to exert greater influence. This is the relationship between a pressure group, a congressional committee and a government department, whereby all three work together for mutual benefit. The agricultural industry in particular has been successful in using iron triangles to achieve greater subsidies for farmers, for example f.

The cause which a group advocates, such as pro- or anti-environmental concerns, or the kind (rich or poor) or number (many or few) of members that it represents can also have a great influence on its success, e.g. the NAACP, representing black Americans, helped bring about the *Brown* v *Board of Topeka* Supreme Court case in 1954, boosting the success of the Civil Rights Movement a.

(Run out of time. Please see bullet points.)

- Media attention to the group, especially if popular, can boost the success of the campaign. Illegal activity can worsen it, e.g. attacks on abortion clinics by pro-life groups in the 1990s a b.
- Good leadership, e.g. Charlton Heston, former leader of NRA a.
- Good organisation, e.g. organising successful campaigns such as the Million Mom March against guns a b.
- Timing and circumstances, e.g. a poor economy making governments less likely to listen to environmental groups such as the Sierra Club wishing to curb industry a b.
- A group's use of modern technology, e.g. Christian Coalition successfully used e-mails and phones to rally support to lobby politicians a b.
- Conclusion g — success depends on a range of factors, circumstances, party in power, strength of membership, whether seen by public as a good cause, all of which are subject to change, therefore changing fortunes of different pressure groups at different times.

(e) a This is a very well-argued, analytical response to the question, with some very impressive AO1 evidence communicated of both success and the lack of it. b A clear focus is maintained throughout, apart from c a slight drift into campaign finance at the beginning, wasting time which could have been used to finish the essay in continuous prose. The essay shows a clear understanding and AO2 analysis of pressure group politics and variable success, with impressive examples well communicated and integrated into the response. d References to Enron and 'cash for access' are particularly impressive as is e knowledge of pressure group numbers of the AARP and the NRA. Political concepts are used, such as f iron triangles, and AO2 links are made to party ideology and pressure group success. The result is an A-grade response, despite the final important and focused arguments and g conclusion being bullet-pointed, which would lower the potential communication (AO3) mark.

(b) There are certain factors with the USA that make some pressure groups more successful than others. First, one of the most obvious is the actual issue in question. A pressure group that promotes a sympathetic issue is more likely to attain success, as it will gain more public and media attention. For example, the National Right to Life pressure group campaigns on the issue of abortion, a subject that is hotly debated in the USA, which allows them to attain more success **a**.

Furthermore, finance is an issue that has a massive role within the US pressure group system. Pressure groups use political action committees to elect and defeat candidates, fund attack adverts and so on. These PACs are highly professional and highly organised in the political marketplace. They bid for power and success within US politics, and ultimately the pressure groups that can 'buy' the best congressmen enjoy the most success. For example, Bush was coined the 'Toxic Texan' due to his links with the oil industry **b**.

However, the Christian Coalition and the American Association of Retired Persons do not use PACs, as finance is not considered a major player in pressure group politics. Both the Christian Coalition and the AARP have mass membership, which is seen as more influential than money. The AARP has a membership of 33 million, which is used to threaten politicians (note that voting turnout among 'grey voters' is extremely high). Politicians cannot afford to lose such massive chunks of voters, especially as US elections are becoming closer and closer (*Bush* v *Gore* in 2000, for instance), and therefore these pressure groups gain massive influence and success **b**.

Furthermore, the system of federalism in the USA creates numerous 'pressure points' where pressure groups can campaign and lobby. They can campaign at local, state and national level, which allows for a great deal of success.

Although the above suggests finance is not a major player in the US pressure group system, pressure groups often hire professional lobbyists to lobby the government on behalf of their cause, often ex-congressmen. Pressure groups that can afford to 'buy' ex-congressmen who have a lot of insight within US government often see a great amount of success **b**.

Furthermore, with the issue of success comes the issue of iron triangles. Iron triangles are the relationship between the interest group, a congressional committee and a government department, an example being the military iron triangle or the agricultural one. These relationships are regarded as being undemocratic, as deals are made without taking into account the interests of society at large. These 'special relationships' are not open to all pressure groups, yet interests such as healthcare and tobacco enjoy such privileges. Gaining such an access point to the government **b** is extremely advantageous to pressure groups and inevitably leads to a great deal of success.

Another factor that can cause US pressure groups a great deal of success is events. After the Sandy Hook shootings and Obama's attempts to pass some restrictions on buying guns, the National Rifle Association (NRA) faced trouble. Yet they campaigned that if guns were widely available someone could have shot the killers before mass murder took place. This event, although damaging to the NRA, in fact publicised its cause.

Finally with regard to the NRA, its success lies in the fact that guns are seen as part of the constitutional right in the USA to bear arms. With the constitution behind it, no politician dares challenge it b.

In conclusion, there are various factors that lead to disproportionate levels of success within US pressure groups.

e b This answer, although quite focused and containing some relevant AO2 analysis, such as the success of the NRA and iron triangles, suffers because many arguments are not developed enough for high AO2 marks: for example, the relationships between access points and success or between publicity and success are not clearly expressed, lowering potential AO2 and AO3 marks, and are not consistently backed up with supporting evidence and examples, such as how and why professional lobbyists can lead to success or how 'events' can lead to success. There is knowledge of PACs but little analysis of their impact on 'success'. There are some contradictions and some lack of logic in the answer regarding the role of finance in pressure group success, as well as some vague and over-generalised assertions, such as a that campaigning at different levels or 'hotly debated' issues or media attention leads to success. The conclusion is also brief. Overall this leads to a C rather than a B grade, with more marks being given for AO1 than for AO2 or AO3.

Knowledge check answers

1 As well as federal elections there are also elections at state (and local) levels of government. This, coupled with the separation of executive and legislative powers, leads to elections for both the executive and legislative branches of both layers of government, creating a long and complex electoral process that may lead to democratic overload and voter fatigue.

2 Caucus selection is mainly used in more rural states and is dominated by the base of politically active, registered party supporters likely to be more liberal in the Democratic Party and more conservative in the Republican Party. This means that candidates will run somewhat ideologically different campaigns in these states, to the left in the Democrat caucuses and the right in the Republican. The Iowa caucus in particular, therefore, is not always a reliable predictor of who is going to win.

3 The 'invisible primary' is the period when candidates declare their intention to run, visiting early-voting states usually a year before the first primary vote. They jostle for position as the front runner, to gain momentum through media attention, increasing name and face recognition and campaign donations. Candidates fade or drop out if they cannot achieve these. The 'winner' of the invisible primary is not guaranteed to win the nomination, so it is not always 'significant' in predicting the winner.

4 The long and extremely gruelling nature of the primaries can be likened to Darwin's 'survival of the fittest'. Only the candidates suited to what will be the gruelling nature of running the executive branch will survive the tests that primaries force upon candidates to prove that they are capable of winning the presidency. Weaker candidates will drop out or be defeated along the way because they do not have what it takes to win.

5 Primaries are divisive contests where the party candidates attack each other to win voter support, as the attacks on Obama by Hillary Clinton showed in 2008, so the party can appear disunited by the time of the convention. Voters dislike divided parties, shown by the Republican Party's 1992 defeat after a bruising primary contest between G. Bush and Pat Buchanon. So in order to present a 'united front' at the convention, 'political wounds' have to be healed through speeches and visible support.

6 The Democratic Party Hunt Commission introduced super-delegates in 1984 to bring an element of 'peer review' into the nomination process. Approximately 20% of convention delegates are not committed by primary or caucus vote. They are the party's hierarchy and elected officials who can vote for whichever candidate they think would be best for the party. They have never influenced the selection because the winner has always had enough delegates to win outright, but they could be significant in a very close race.

7 Presidential campaigns are run by paid, professional political consultants who determine the strategy and tactics of the campaign. Candidates rely on such advisers to help them win, such as Clinton's reliance on James Carville, G. W. Bush's on Karl Rove and Obama's on David Axelrod. There are also pollsters, media advisers and spin doctors who make up the campaign team of 'hired guns', which is one reason why so much money is needed for campaigns.

8 Modern electoral campaigns focus on 'marketing' the candidates themselves and their media image rather than the party or policies, leading to highly personalised campaigns and specialist advisers working for candidates rather than parties. This is criticised as focusing on more trivial 'style' factors such as likeability and how candidates look rather than serious policy issues of substance.

9 Candidates try to gain as much 'free media' as possible through photo-opportunities or newsworthy events, to get their campaigns into the broadcast media and news, increasing name and face recognition without using precious campaign finance to pay for publicity. This is contrasted with advertising that must be paid for in expensive television slots. Most campaign money is spent on these paid commercials, especially on prime-time television in key states.

10 After FECA, most presidential candidates accepted federal funding for their campaigns. However, with escalating campaign costs, wealthy candidates who have amassed large war chests are now more likely to reject such funding and the spending limits that come with it. Bush and Kerry rejected federal funding in 2004, as did Obama in 2008 despite originally saying that he would accept it. As a result he had a huge financial advantage over McCain, who accepted $84 million of federal funds. Obama's decision resulted from a spectacularly successful fund-raising campaign through the internet and social media.

11 The 1st Amendment guarantees freedom of speech, which extends, according to the Supreme Court, to spending in support of, or opposing, candidates through 'independent expenditures' (so-called 'political speech'). So it is impossible to restrict campaign finance when individuals or organisations can legally donate unlimited sums of money to independent groups such as the 527s and Super PACs to use for 'issue advocacy' or to fund their own campaigns.

12 This rare event occurs because the Electoral College has a winner-takes-all system in 48 out of 50 states. This means a candidate can win a state by a small margin of votes but then receive all that state's EC votes, as Bush did in Florida in 2000 with only 547 votes more than Gore, but gaining all the state's 27 EC votes. Votes for a candidate can also pile up in safe states but are only adding to the popular vote total. So the popular vote can be high but just not won in places where it counts.

13 'Faithless' electors who fail to vote for the candidate who won their state's popular vote have occurred in six elections since 1960, with nothing to prevent this constitutionally. They have little significance because individual 'rogue' electors have never had any impact on the outcome of a presidential election, usually just making some political point of their own, but they could be highly significant in a tied or very close EC vote.

14 The mechanism of the EC arises directly from its origins within a federal state with jealously guarded states' rights. It is the 50 states that elect the president, based on their state representation in Congress (plus DC), and this suits both small and large states for different reasons, so they would be unlikely to vote to change this system through a constitutional amendment.

15 Direct democracy mechanisms are simply an 'add on' to the normal decision-making process in the legislatures of the states that use them. The majority of state decisions are made after debate and deliberation by representatives taking decisions on behalf of the people whom they were elected to represent. Referendums and initiatives are not replacing but supplementing this process.

16 Referendums originate from state legislatures, which may decide to consult the voters for approval or disapproval, either before or after making a decision. They are top down because they are put to the people. Initiatives originate from the people themselves attempting to put a proposition onto the ballot paper through signature petitions in their states and so are described as bottom up (although the process may have been 'hijacked' by special interests).

17 Direct democracy devices are triggered by gathering petition signatures from registered voters in order to place a question on the ballot paper. Because states decide their own decision-making processes, this will vary between states. The number of signatures needed relates to the voter turnout at the last election and is usually between 5 and 15% of that voting population to prevent frivolous and frequent ballot petitions.

18 The term 'realignment' refers to fundamental changes to the electoral coalitions supporting the parties, leading to a change in party dominance because of shifts in voting behaviour, as seen during the Great Depression in the 1930s and the elections of that period. Since then there has been no sign of either a permanent Republican or Democrat majority appearing. However, the South realigned to the Republican Party in the 1960s and the 'solid' Democrat South is now a Republican stronghold.

19 The New Deal Coalition of votes that gave the Democratic Party majority party status from the 1930s to the 1960s (bar the Eisenhower presidency) broke down under the pressure of internal contradictions where the conservative, white southern voters who had supported the party since the civil war voted for the same party as the more liberal minority, blue-collar and radical intellectual voters from the northern states. The party's move to support civil rights and lifestyle changes in the 1960s led to the breakaway of the white South and some conservative blue-collar workers from this voting coalition.

20 There remains a fairly wide range of opinions and diversity within the Democrat Party, even though it has become more liberal and shed most of its more conservative elements since the 1970s. 'Blue dogs' favour a more moderate and conservative approach to policies such as healthcare reform and redistribution of wealth via progressive taxation. They are also more likely to resist major efforts at gun control and widening the availability of abortion. New Democrats also favour a fiscally conservative policy, but are more liberal on social policies, such as abortion and gay rights. Progressive Democrats are the most liberal faction within the party, and are strongly in favour of greater expenditure on social security to try to reduce the wealth inequality in the USA. They also favour stricter gun laws and tend to be the strongest opponents of overseas military intervention.

21 In the 1994 mid-term election the Republican Party, under the leadership of Newt Gingrich, stood under the banner of the Contract with America — in effect, a national manifesto proposing very conservative policy positions such as a balanced budget to win the House for the Republicans. This 'manifesto', part of the 'Republican Revolution', led to a clearly more ideologically conservative Republican Party under speaker Gingrich, although most of the proposals did not pass or were vetoed by Clinton.

22 Democrats favour activist, federal government intervention in the economy and greater regulation, as they believe that only the federal government can create more fair and equal conditions as seen in the New Deal and Great Society programmes, Obama's healthcare reforms and regulation of the banks. Republicans, in contrast, favour little government intervention in the free market, creating incentives for individuals to work harder and the private sector to create jobs with less regulation and smaller, more limited government, balanced budgets and states' rights.

23 Because of rising deficits, bailouts and stimulus intervention started by Bush and continued by Obama, the Tea Party movement started to press for changes to the economic direction of the country and greater fiscal conservatism. The movement has pushed the Republican Party further to the right, seen in the Tea Party candidates in the 2010 mid-terms, the influence on the 2012 primaries and the Republican agenda generally, perhaps alienating more moderate Republicans in the process.

24 In the federal USA, parties are organised at state level and operate under state law. They are de-centralised in structure with little if any control by the national party through the DNC and RNC, unlike the centralised, national UK parties. This means that there are big differences between state parties depending on the state and its characteristics. The state parties only meet every 4 years when their delegates attend the nominating conventions. Therefore, the USA is said to have a 50- or 100-party system with each party being different in the 50 states.

25 In a two-party-dominated political system, third parties' only chance of making an impact would be to have some influence on the political agenda of the time or the outcome of a single election. Most are short-lived and based around individual candidates and single issues that are often ignored by the two main parties, such as Wallace in 1968 (civil rights), Perot in 1992 and 1996 (budget deficits) and Nader in 2000 and 2004 (environmental issues). However, though votes can be gained by these third-party candidates and issues can be raised, most fail to survive and benefit simply from short-term protest votes.

26 States are described as 'red' (Republican) or 'blue' (Democrat) because of their loyalty to one or other of the parties. This is because states have very different social, ethnic, racial and demographic features within them. The red Republican states are mainly the more rural/suburban states in the South or the Midwest, such as Utah or Alabama, with a majority of Republican voters, and the blue states are the more liberal Northeast states such as Massachusetts and Vermont, socially and ethnically diverse states such as California and the more industrial states such as Illinois. Some

'swing' states, however, have a more 'purple mix' within them and are not dominated by one party.

27 Unlike the UK, which developed from a feudal system with a defined social hierarchy and where it is said that 'class is the basis of voting behaviour', the USA lacks a sense of class consciousness with over 90% of Americans defining themselves as 'middle class' through lifestyle. In the USA, other divisions such as race, ethnicity, religion and region are more significant in explaining political identity, attitudes and voting behaviour.

28 The black vote has been heavily Democrat since the 1930s and the Democratic Party therefore feels it does not have to win over this group of voters by making appeals specifically to them. The Republican Party, achieving only 5% of the black vote in 2008, knows there is little point appealing to voters it cannot win.

29 Hispanics are the largest growing minority in the USA and their vote is significant in many battleground states with high Electoral College votes. Largely Spanish speaking and Catholic, their vote has been 'up for grabs' in recent elections where many were energised to vote by the moral values focus of the Republicans in 2004 and the more favourable views on immigration and welfare of the Democrats in 2008. As their numbers increase, both parties will target them as a key group of voters to win over.

30 Older voters are more likely to turn out to vote in elections than younger voters, as they have a stronger partisan alignment and feel it is their democratic duty to vote. As a result their interests are more likely to be focused on by parties seeking to maximise votes, such as prescription drug benefits or healthcare and support in old age.

31 Two examples of voters with cross-cutting identifications would be: a Hispanic, Catholic, male, chief executive living in the suburbs of Chicago in Illinois; and an unmarried female, white Protestant living in a rural area in Kansas and working as a civil servant in the public sector. There are many other combinations that can illustrate the difficulties of predicting the way a person is going to vote based solely on social characteristics.

32 In the 2004 presidential election the issues that dominated the election were moral values focusing on abortion and gay marriage and also national security issues as this was the first election after 9/11 and the War on Terror. In 2012 the main issue was the ongoing state of the economy, following the bank bailouts and the stimulus package. It was also an opportunity to judge Obama's first term in office.

33 Be careful here, for while it is true that voter turnout is significantly lower than it was say 50 years ago, turnout has increased slightly recently. It rose in 2008 and only fell back slightly in 2012. It is perhaps fairer to say that turnout has on the whole fallen over the last 30–40 years, but reached its lowest point in 1996, and has picked up somewhat since then. In part, this is the result of laws such as HAVA, but above all perhaps due to the relatively close nature of some recent elections.

34 Voter turnout rises and falls at different elections depending on the engagement of the electorate and the successful mobilisation of the vote. The lowest turnout was in 1996 with

53% of eligible voters voting (49% of VAP) whilst the highest turnout was 64% of eligible voters in 2008. Fluctuations relate to the different candidates and voters' perceptions of them and the dominating issues that differ at each election as well as how close the election is seen to be.

35 Countervailing groups (or lobbies) are those which oppose or counteract one another on a specific issue, providing some degree at least of pressure group balance. Examples are the 'pro-choice' (NARAL Pro-Choice America or Planned Parenthood) and 'pro-life' groups (National Right to life) on the issue of abortion, and pro- (National Rifle Association) and anti- (Handgun Control Inc) gun control groups.

36 These are groups organised around, and advocating for, a single issue as opposed to multiple issues. Examples are groups such as the gun lobby, the NRA, groups focused on protecting the environment such as the Sierra Club and the Jewish lobby AIPAC, focused on pro-Israel policy. Single-issue lobbies can be fanatical and intense in their focus and activities, such as 'pro-life' groups on the issue of abortion.

37 In contrast to the UK, the Supreme Court's power of constitutional interpretation and judicial review makes it an important access point for pressure groups that wish to influence its decisions in areas connected to their interest or cause. As a result, groups like the NAACP and ACLU submit amicus curiae briefs, sponsor litigation in test cases and try and influence the nomination and confirmation processes for Supreme Court justices when a vacancy arises, to try to influence the selection of either judicially 'liberal' or 'conservative' justices.

38 Pressure groups try to influence the election of politicians sympathetic to their interest or cause, or alternatively try to negatively target those who oppose them for defeat. They can make hard money contributions to campaigns through PACs, or 'spend on behalf of' using issue advocacy, which since the Citizens United case has been unrestricted, and has led to the rise of Super PACs. They do this because they would like to gain access to politicians if they win or to remove politicians who may oppose their aims and objectives.

39 The revolving door spins or recycles politicians and officials out of elected or appointed office and into lucrative positions in lobbying organisations usually in the K Street Corridor, after a 2-year 'cooling off' period brought about by the Honest Leadership and Open Government Act of 2007. It can be argued that this is an abuse of public service and potentially corrupt as they are exploiting insider contacts and expertise gained when in office for monetary gain. Three out of four oil and gas lobbyists previously worked in the federal government.

40 PACs are criticised because their 'hard money' campaign contributions to electoral candidates, which are often 'bundled', lead to a perception that politicians can be 'bought' and that you have to 'pay to play'. It is feared that PAC contributions may influence the voting intentions of elected politicians, who are elected to represent their constituents not pressure groups with PACs. However, there is little evidence of any clear link between PAC contributions and roll call votes in Congress.

Note: **bold** page numbers indicate definitions of key terms.

AQA A2 Government & Politics